WHAT ARE YOU SAYING ...?

... and why you are not saying it

CONOR KENNY

Published by Oak Tree Press, Cork T12 EVT0, Ireland

www.oaktreepress.com / www.SuccessStore.com

© 2020 Conor Kenny

A catalogue record of this book is available from the British Library.

ISBN 978 1 78119 446 1 (Paperback)

ISBN 978 1 78119 447 8 (ePub)

ISBN 978 1 78119 448 5 (Kindle)

ISBN 978 1 78119 4449 2 (PDF)

Cover illustration: iulika1 / 123rf.com

Cover design: Kieran O'Connor Design

CONTENTS

DEDICATION

This book is about how we communicate and how we impact on other people. It is a book based on my own experience. Experience shapes us, and we are defined by it. It moulds us into who we are and how we are perceived. Our impact can last a lifetime.

Naturally, the first influences come from family and, especially, a wider family. Each generation can teach you something and so this book is also dedicated to: Ivor, Maureen, Ann, Judith, Dermot, Geraldine, Helen, Rob, Mark, Nathalie, Ivor, Maeve, Grace, Dermot, Alex, Christopher, Matthew, Gabrielle and Edward.

As we grow from childhood into life, love, and careers, we look back and begin to understand the events and kindness that profoundly influenced our future. We reflect on those pivotal and defining moments. We reflect on tough lessons and happy days. We label them as memories, but they run deeper. They make us who we are, for better, for worse.

At 15 years of age, I went to boarding school.

Mount St. Joseph's Abbey, Roscrea, is a beautiful place sitting on over 1,000 acres of prime midland countryside. At 15, it was not beautiful; it was lonely, isolated, and frightening. I saw it as an open detention centre. In hindsight, it was the best thing that ever happened to me and my two years there left the deepest positive mark.

To this day, and very often, I walk Mount St. Joseph's grounds with my close friend Vincent, a former student too. We ramble in walks and words, but we are always happy there. I questioned this once and his reply flowed:

It was always beautiful, Conor. But now, you can leave any time you want to.

That is the difference and the legacy it left.

This book is dedicated to Norman Davey, a former teacher at the Cistercian College at Mount St. Joseph's An understated gentleman, it is important that he, along with every dedicated teacher, knows how precious their work is and how they influence our path for the rest of our lives. This book is also dedicated to the wider monastic community at Mount St. Joseph's, along with the devoted teachers and people who moved my thinking from here to there.

We owe great teachers a great debt.

Acknowledgements

Without the support, patience, and expertise of these special people, I could not have authored this book:

- Grace Gallagher, who has worked with me for 15 years to help build our small entrepreneurial castle. Without time off and her encouragement to begin another book, there would be no book;

- Vincent O'Brien, my lifelong friend, and expert in living life through a never-ending bubble of happiness. His microscopic observations always spotted the flaws;

- Mark Kenny, my brother. He coined the title when I got stuck;

- Brian O'Kane, who I have worked with on all four of my books. He is patient and challenging and devoted to producing the best and squeezing the author to be the best.

I am forever indebted to these extraordinary and vital people. In their own quiet way, they have left an indelible mark. This is their book too.

Introduction

Do you understand? I don't want you to do a thing if you don't understand it.

Kristin Cashore

I Do Not Understand What You Are Saying

There is always a temptation to focus on something sounding good rather than being understood. The first is tempting; the second works. Trying to be the next Wordsworth is not a good idea.

The next time you are in a busy city, look at how many vans are emblazoned with the word 'Solutions'. Some proclaim to 'Sell solutions' and I hear you ask, "Solutions to what?" Like you, I have no idea. That is the problem.

One of the most meaningless and overused phrases in marketing is 'magical'. A quick look at the Oxford English Dictionary provides a definition:

Mysterious tricks, such as making things disappear and reappear, performed as entertainment. The power of influencing events by using mysterious or supernatural forces.

I was delivering a communications and marketing workshop. There were 20 business owners. A challenge, given that each ran a different business and each had a thirst for more knowledge, and humbling to see successful people, well into their middle life, working so hard to learn.

Like every group, there was a mix of personalities.

One stood out.

He was young, loud, and proud.

The wonderful zest of youth had yet to teach him the finer skills of patience, curbing exuberance, and listening.

At the beginning, I asked people to write down the shortest possible version of their message. In seconds, from the back of the room came a loud "Done".

Working my way around the tables, there was a mixture of good to fair. Not a bad start. They were moving into the right space to reimagine their message.

Now, it was his turn. He stood up to amplify an immensely proud message:

"We sell magical experiences."

I thanked him.

The day went on and we worked together to refine and sharpen their marketing, words and messages.

As we ended, I asked everyone to write their message again, based on what they had learnt throughout the day. This is the reward for all their effort and their messages had moved successfully from east to west.

Except for one.

I invited him to deliver the latest version of his message, based on all we had discussed. He did:

"We sell magical experiences."

A few seats away was a diligent young woman who had worked hard all day. She had transformed a very ordinary message into something compelling and clear. The young man had irritated her and the dam burst.

Fixing her eyes on him, she said, "You are still selling magical experiences? That is what you said early this morning. I do not understand".

He was not about to let go and replied using the same line again.

Quick as a flash, she said, "Great, can I have one magical experience now? And perhaps you can wrap one for me to take away as well?"

He looked confused and said, "I do not understand what you mean".

She replied, "Exactly my point".

Words

What you see and what you hear depends on where you stand.

Skilful writing, clear dialogue and effective engagement is like someone looking in the mirror trying to decide whether they are good-looking. Unless they are smothering on an oversized ego, it is not something we can answer. Communication is a bit like that. Did we connect or did we simply think we connected?

In 1982 the Tunisian-born French singer F.R. David sold over eight million copies of his hit single *Words,* summing up what each of us wrestle with at different times:

Words don't come easy to me.
How can I find a way to make you see I love you?
Words don't come easy.

Words are like drugs. Addictive and dangerous, healing, and evocative.

Words hurt; words heal. They can light fires and cause tears. They can bring terror or bring relief – but, strangely, words are always neutral. How we interpret and understand them; well, that is a different matter.

This book is not really about words; it is more than that. It is about how we send and how we receive. It is about what we say, how we say it and most of all, it is about making sure that what you wanted to communicate is what is received.

Misinterpretation is not the same thing as being confused.

If you are confused and resolve the riddle, then confusion is the right path to learning and knowledge. It is good.

Misinterpretation or, if you like, misunderstanding means believing you have understood something when you have not. You just think you have. It is a sign that leads to the wrong address. It is not good.

How we communicate is a complex mix of many things: our upbringing, our influences, our values, our fears, our goals, what we want and more. It is that potent combination of emotion and facts that creates the potential for many mirages and optical illusions.

This book is in no way tells you what to do. Instead, it reflects my own interest, what I have learnt, what I have shared over many years of writing and speaking and, of course, the lessons that three earlier books have taught me about authoring this book.

Whilst many might call me an extrovert, that is half the story. The other half, the introvert, adores watching people interact, communicate, listen, engage and so on. How many times have you and I watched a dialogue only to conclude that neither party were listening? How often have we witnessed the clash of egos rather than arguing the issue? How many times have we written something, sent it off and instantly wished we had not? How often did we know what we wanted to say but just could not get it out? How many times did we beat and punish ourselves for rushing and shipping it too fast?

Writing is simply one tool to communicate and, for me, one I feel most at ease with to say what I want to say. It is my personal comfort zone and founded only on one thing – the desire to be understood.

In this book, I want to share stories – true stories – of my own journey to being more aware of how we arrive at being understood. It would be tempting to say 'How we communicate' but that is shallow. The only goal in any interaction is simply to be understood. That gives the reader, the listener, or the decision maker a choice. That is fair. Once they have that clear picture, you can do no more.

My hope is that this book will help you avoid tying your feet together before you start to run.

Conor Kenny
September 2020

1 : Why We Communicate

Communicating is loud and silent, obvious, and subtle. It is a complex transmission of signals that we intuitively piece together to deliver a message that we feel we need to convey.

It includes silence, noise, domination, submission, listening, not listening, writing, words, voice, tone, eyes, posture and more.

It is also not something we stop to think about too often – though we should.

Six Reasons

Communication happens for a reason and can be thought of as always falling into six types:

- **To inform:** This means to bring information to another that we believe they need and may not have – think newspapers or an operating manual;

- **To inspire or motivate:** This means to bring a future idea to life, to get agreement, buy in or even just enjoy dreaming about it – think about the conversation we might have about starting a new business;

- **To influence or persuade:** The goal is to alter someone's thinking, for better, for worse – think of the sales professional;

- **To conform to expectations:** This is how we see ourselves and helps us communicate in a social way that conforms to that norm – think of a party linked to work or with your friends;

- **To set up new connections:** This means how we connect to grow and develop a network;

- **To enjoy:** For many, conversation is enjoyable, motivational, relaxing, distracting and simply playful fun – think of coffee with friends and meeting colleagues you like.

The Philosopher

Like many very average university students in my year, studying and lectures were an annoying distraction that got in the way of far more important matters, like having an enjoyable time. But, even with a young mind that passionately believed that life was simple, and we all already know as much as we need, in later life some nuggets have stuck.

I majored in philosophy, the love of wisdom, and fundamental questions about existence, knowledge, values, reason, the mind, and language. Ironic for a guy bent on bliss rather than lectures.

In first year, about 300 students took it as their easy third subject. By our final year, the honours class had shed 286 philosophers and only 14 of us battled, debated, and imagined our way through the works of Plato, Aristotle, Russell, Kant, and Jean Paul Sartre.

I could understand Sartre and only fragments of highly interesting and deeply confusing theories about proving things that were impossible to prove. As students, this was not so much about agreeing an answer but everything to do with enjoying debate and persuasion. In many ways, philosophy is raising its head again in the undertones of this book and, after all these years, coming full circle. Its footprint has never gone away.

Role Play

Back to Jean Paul Sartre. This is the man who gave us his view of the world in one tiny comment:

Hell is other people.

This famous statement conjures up the image of an easily-irritated, introverted curmudgeon. That is not the case; it is a misunderstanding of context. In fact, what he was saying was pointing out our own loss of freedom if we surrender to needing the approval of others.

Easy to misunderstand and easy to pass judgement. The wrong judgement.

Though I learnt much from that famous line, I learnt more from another Sartre theory.

Sartre believed that we all share an image of ourselves that we are almost predestined to follow. He describes our inevitable tumble into the character we adopt and often we express that in the career we choose.

If we choose to be an architect, it's only time before we adopt the dress code of an architectural practice. If we become the Maître D' of a fine restaurant, it would not take long before our language had a hint of international tones, a whiff of superiority and a flirt with assumed extreme confidence.

His point is simply that we play out the role of what we believe ourselves to be and follow the code of communication that goes with that.

How we see ourselves, how we position ourselves in life and in work, will determine how we communicate.

Let me give you an example of how our self-image twists around to fit that imaginary ideal.

Who We Want to Be and Why Jimmy Became James

I knew Jimmy from my youth. We were typical average students from anonymous but nice, leafy suburbs. Like every teenager of that time, we had our own circle. It was an ordinary circle with no outstanding achievers, and little separated us.

As time goes by, we drift into new circles and actively stay connected with a smaller group from teenage days. Often, with the passage of time, greying of hair and loss of athletic figures, it can be a shock to meet again. In our mind, they were blessed with eternal youth.

I was invited to a small party. In came Jimmy, a former member of our little group. I was looking forward to chatting with him after so many years. Jimmy looked the same, no grey hair and a handsome man who carried himself well. Eventually, we got talking. I had lived in London for nine years and it certainly had not changed me. Jimmy was in London for just one now and it had changed him.

Naturally, I greeted him with fondness, "Hi Jimmy, great to see you after all this time". He flung an icy stare back and said, "James, not Jimmy". His attractive new British wife joined in with an accent straight from Buckingham Palace. Her handshake was regal, and her behaviour matched. Jimmy was never ever known as James and a few eyebrows ascended to heaven. I persisted, curious how Jimmy turned into James. It was then that I got caught in a rapid choice of whether to burst out into uncontrollable laughter or pretend false understanding.

I chose the latter.

After some superficial chit-chat ,I asked James where he was living in London. The answer came quickly under the supervision of his new wife: "Key – Ann – Sing – Tun".

I was confused. The pronunciation was deliberate, slow, and controlled. I had no idea where he was talking about. I was confused.

"Jimmy, sorry, I mean James, where exactly did you say you were living again?"

This time, James spoke a little quicker and I got it. He was living in Kensington. Jimmy wanted to be James. It was his vision of himself and he was brave enough to go there.

And that is the starting point for how we are going to communicate and behave into the future.

We decide, we adopt, and we become.

2: THE PROBLEM WITH COMMUNICATION

If I had to select only one quotation that would help people communicate more effectively, it would be this:

The single biggest problem in communication is the illusion that it has taken place.

George Bernard Shaw

We believe, even assume, that what we intended to say was what was received. That is the illusion and often, not the case. The danger is simple: you will not be understood. Inevitably, that creates an unnecessary problem in any setting you can think of.

The goal is always the same: to make sure that what you want someone to understand is what they understand.

Going to the Moon

It was one of those rare pleasant mid-summer nights. Late enough to have no plans, too early to surrender to the night. My good friend Vincent called. He was not ready to stop for the day either.

"There is a mountain an hour away that has beautiful flint stones that are almost pure white. Shall we go collect some for our gardens?"

It was not so much about the art of landscaping but two young men squeezing the last drop from a beautiful day.

We arrived into this heavenly corner as the last light started to fade. The sky was clear, and the first stars were like centurions coming to finish off the slivers of colourful streaming light. A battle only one would win. Time was against us. There was work to be done.

It was an exceptionally beautiful place and seeing nature settling down for the night was special. With the darkness came the quiet.

We walked up and up and up not sure where these abundant rocks were lying. As if they knew we were seeking them out, they were disguised under a thin layer of camouflaged green. Push it aside and their brilliance was striking. Like diamonds, a little polishing revealed their beauty.

We got increasingly selective and, in the pursuit of excellence, feasting on this sparkling crop, we pushed higher and higher towards the mountaintop.

Vincent was about 100 metres ahead foraging away on a very steep slope near the summit. The mountain was narrowing, and a slope had become a wall. I was on lower ground admiring the dusky view and watching the stars gathering in numbers and power.

Just behind the mountain's peak, out of nowhere, the moon started to rise. I had never seen anything like it before and never since. It was enormous and the perfect balance of light showed up every detail. It was the most marvellous sight of nature doing its thing.

From where I stood, I watched its rapid ascent and growing size. It looked like a giant light bulb inside a free-floating translucent balloon.

In the middle of nowhere, voices carry easily. From a distance, I shouted up to Vincent: "Look at the moon, it is amazing".

Vincent looked up and could see nothing other than the occasional star and fast-fading light. He was a man on a mission, a flint stone mission. "What are you talking about? I see stars, no moon. Are you imagining things?"

I told him it was directly above his head, enormous, rising fast and it looked like he was carrying it on his shoulders.

A practical man, Vincent was convinced that my earlier rock-hauling had taken me into a world of hallucinogenic astronomy. With a hint of impatience came: "Yeah, right, the moon. Not a star, a big moon. You keep looking for the moon. I will keep looking for white rocks".

There was no convincing him. I gave up.

Twenty minutes later, full of rocks and empty of energy, we descended slowly to our car. Our mission accomplished.

Vincent turned around to look back at our midnight mountain. "My God, look at the moon, it is unreal."

I resisted the urge to say, "I told you so".

Instead, I said, "I guess when your nose was against the rock face on the steepest part of the mountain, you could not see what I saw?"

He laughed, avoided the answer, put his arm on my shoulder and started to sing Frank Sinatra's *Fly Me to The Moon*.

And that is what the opening line of this book means:

What you see and what you hear depends on where you stand.

She Suffered Memory Loss

Beauty is truth and truth beauty, that is all ye know on earth and all ye need to know.

John Keats

Communication can easily be distorted by memory or even memory loss.

Memory can trick us. The further back it goes, the more it can be embroidered and there is always the danger that our memory is a memory of the last version of the memory and ends up being a long way from what happened. If we are honest with ourselves, we might realise that 'truth' can have many versions, but truth is neutral, it is our memory that adds colour and spice.

We took on a one-day assignment to work through a little impasse within a management team who had tied themselves up in a nasty knot and needed untangling.

The brief and the outcome they wanted were clear and a pathway to arriving at the solution was agreed in advance.

The day was done, and the goal comfortably reached. Politics and positioning had allowed innuendo to become fact and the landscape was distorted forever through a false prism. We corrected that.

Sometime later, a very strange phone call came. The woman who had commissioned the work was not happy. Not only was it unusual to hear this, it simply did not make sense since the documented facts spoke for

1 1

themselves. But, if that is how someone feels, then it is right to listen carefully and understand their perspective.

The call got increasingly challenging and the facts were entering a state of high distortion and imagined events.

Still, I listened patiently.

In the end, having vented emotionally, she concluded a lengthy and sometimes strange monologue with: "And I trust my colleagues. I trust them implicitly and they would not tell me that it was just OK if that was not the case. In retrospect, having listened to my colleagues, I am sorry I did not make myself available to attend. Now what do you have to say to all of that?"

Throughout the monologue, I recalled all the feedback notes praising the day universally. I gently reminded her that the evidence was contrary to the recollection.

She said, "Give me an example".

I read out three and then she stopped me. Facts and imagination were clearly clashing but I insisted on reading one more. It was lavish and congratulatory.

When I finished reading it to her, she said, "That is a little over the top but that is their perspective."

Then this young dynamic woman in a hurry asked the important and inevitable question: "Can you tell me who wrote that?".

I said it would be my pleasure. I deliberately paused to make sure the impact of what I was about to say struck an indelible chord.

"You."

There was silence and then I added, "You were there that day too. All day. You thanked me, in your words, for a wonderful day".

It would be easy to ridicule this young woman afor a simple mistake but that would be unfair.

Her team were all older than her and I could see their resentment of her high office, even though it was well-disguised.

And what had happened? They had played a game with her and set a trap. The intention was simply to destabilise her.

The only mistake she made was to believe a much-distorted version of the reality but, at that moment, it was her belief, her perspective and what we believe in that moment is our reality.

And what did I admire the most?

A week later, a beautiful hand-written note and a bottle of fine wine arrived. The note said, "I am so sorry for rushing to judgement and allowing the truth to be distorted. A lesson learnt. Thank you for being honest".

That took courage, a quality always worth admiring no matter how bumpy the landing.

The Three Patricks

If ever you have got your car stuck in thick mud or even snow, you will know what I mean. The instinct is to accelerate, hoping you will terrorise the car into a startled gallop and break free. Logic tells us otherwise. The desire to put the boot down simply creates a bigger hole and a bigger problem.

There is always a defining moment when some light dawns. Like everyone, for our own business, I knew what I wanted to express but whatever route I chose to express it, the outcome was even more confusion. Sometimes, in communication, this is what we do: we dig a deeper more confusing hole. Once these enlightening pivotal moments occur, there is no going back. In the world of communication, my moment happened at a flipchart with the three Patricks.

These three fine gentlemen were people I admired hugely for their achievements, intellect, and outstanding ability to make the complicated appear simple.

I was struggling to express what it is our company does and what it delivers. Ironically, all these years later, it is still so much easier to do this for others.

Padraig Ó Céidigh is one of Ireland's most successful entrepreneurs, business strategists and visionaries. For four years, he was also an independent Senator.

Padraic Gilligan and I go back to our university days. Padraic is one of the finest writers and communicators around.

Patrick Delaney combines that rare ability to see the world through cheerful eyes and only sees a world full of adventure, opportunity and hugs. He and Padraic Gilligan made an enormous impact on the meetings, events, and conference business in Ireland.

13

Looking back, it was a real privilege to have these three men accept my invite to challenge what I was trying to say, even though all three are longstanding friends. I will be forever in their debt.

Padraig asked me a simple question "What do you do?" and I struggled to answer it. As the day went on, the car got stuck deeper and deeper into the mud.

It would be nice to say that, at dusk, I had cracked it, and, between us, we had the most beautiful piece of prose. We did not.

I left even more confused and a little agitated. In the years since, I look back on that selfless giving day where the three Patricks gave up their precious busy time purely to help me polish up my message. Why? Because it lit a fire inside. A fire that says we must be able to express clearly what we mean and make sure that the other person really understands what that message is. We did refine our message eventually and it was a wonderful classroom with a fantastic lesson.

Their generosity indirectly has helped the many businesses we work with today because I am challenging them in the way the three Patricks challenged me and that only has one goal: to make sure we are heard and correctly.

From a Retirement Home to Taking Drugs

It was a dull grey day and I was sitting in slow-moving, wet traffic.

A big billboard caught my eye. Its paper was now rain-soaked and flapping in the wind; its message drew an unconscious sigh. It said, "For a fresh perspective on life and a new outlook on living" accompanied by a close-up image of faded original colours that once depicted something. Its location was a non-descript road with many competing messages. I had no idea what they were selling. In time, I travelled the same road and it was the third occasion before I figured out the photo.

When I am delivering workshops on communication, marketing, and sales, this is precious metal. I read the slogan and ask everyone to write down the answer to what the authors of this slogan were trying to sell.

The answers range from health foods, a day spa, diet classes, night courses, a gym, hypnotherapy, plastic surgery, retirement homes and even drugs.

The answer? They were selling apartments. If the poster had simply said "Really Nice Apartments", then clearly everyone would have understood.

For me, it is far better to grasp the Universe as it really is than to persist in delusion, however satisfying and reassuring.

Carl Sagan

Destroying and Building

Another lesson from our classrooms.

It can be remarkably interesting for some people to understand the finer details of linguistics or even NLP (neuro linguistic programming). However, most of us can only absorb a small amount of learning and lessons in any given lecture. With understanding always the goal and with the belief that much of what we say often lands in a way we had not intended, one word can illustrate the point.

Allow me, in a moment, to throw one word at you. As soon as you read it, in your mind, or on paper, immediately capture and hold on to what that word meant. Do not change the meaning or even analyse it. You cannot be wrong in what I am about to share.

The word is 'buckle'.

No doubt, you produced something like:

- The buckle on a belt – to strengthen and secure.
- The bicycle wheel buckled – to collapse and fail.

Of course, both answers are perfectly correct, but you can now see that one word can instantly conjure up two directly opposite meanings. That means, on average, half the people you wanted to talk to completely misunderstood what you meant.

3: CREATING FEAR

Words mean much more than what we see in text or on paper. It takes our voice to give them deeper meaning. Words are a tool, just like a razor-sharp carving knife. In the right hands, they can do a fantastic job; in the wrong ones, they can kill.

Words are, of course, the most powerful drug used by mankind.

Rudyard Kipling

Each of us are in some way conflicted by our emotions. What frightens me will not frighten you and *vice versa*. Fear is illogical and, though we know that, it is extremely hard to apply logic where fear reigns.

What we rarely know is what the other people fear. We may get occasional glimpses, but we do not know. Unintentionally, we can wreak havoc by the way we communicate. If words are powerful, we must use them carefully. Through your words, you become who you really are and that is who we will meet.

In an earlier book, *Dancing at the Fountain*, I spent time talking with Bernard Murphy, the then Chief Executive of the luxurious Gleneagles Hotel in Scotland. A great listener and enormously understated, Bernard left an impression that continues to echo long after we met.

Although everything he said was interesting, two lines stuck and add depth to our thinking. He was talking about how we treat people.

The first: "Are you doing something to me or are you doing something for me?" sums up the choice we all make when we engage.

The second is clever and powerful: "I don't like the grotty phrase 'treat people the way you want to be treated'. Nonsense. Treat people the way they want to be treated".

My life has been full of terrible misfortunes, most of which never happened.

Michel de Montaigne

What is Fear?

If you are living in fear, you are simply living in your imagination. Imagination is not reality and it is not 'the present moment'. We are lost in the future, lost in the past and lost in our imagination.

Imagination used correctly is amazing; not used wisely, it is dangerous, extremely dangerous. And what do we need to do? Use it positively. Use it well.

If you would like to check how you are using it, try this: if you start every negative thought with "What if?", then it is a sure bet that you are about to suffer and become the victim of your own thinking. Remember, you are living in your imagination but ... believing it is reality. It is not. Only the 'right now' is reality.

When we create fear, we create a problem. When we create a problem, inevitably, we create pain.

It is always a choice and one we should think about first.

What Does That Mean?

A straightforward way to understand fear and the silent voice of challenging mental health issues is to understand cause and effect and Cognitive Behavioural Theory (CBT).

CBT is based on the notion that how we think (cognition), how we feel (emotion) and how we then act (behaviour) all link. That means our thoughts determine our feelings and our feelings create our behaviour.

Who is Albert Ellis?

Albert Ellis was an American psychologist who, in 1955, developed Rational Emotive Behaviour Therapy. He held MA and PhD degrees in clinical psychology from Columbia University and the American Board of Professional Psychology. He also founded and was the President of the New York City-based Albert Ellis Institute for decades. He is one of the originators of the cognitive revolutionary paradigm shift in psychotherapy and an early proponent of cognitive-behavioural therapies (source: Wikipedia).

Ellis took a different approach, looking into how our own thoughts can create so much pain. He believed that we allow our emotions to be dominated by the 'musts':

- "I must be successful";
- "I must be loved";
- "I must have what I want".

He went on to explain this through the A, B, and C of emotion:

- **A** is the activating event (you get turned down for promotion);
- **B** is the belief that follows (I am not good enough);
- **C** is the consequence (I feel like a failure and my mood is low).

Whilst we might understand A easily, it is highly unlikely that we understand or know what happens in points B and C.

That means we have an obligation to tread carefully in what we write, what we say, what we do and how we do it.

Isn't that why fools rush in where angels fear to tread?

Buying Milk in New York – A Trick of the Mind

I have been very privileged in my winding career to have travelled to many countries. Some were dull, some exciting and the rest a mix of both.

New York has an energy an aura that captivates you and always leaves an imprint. London, a city I lived in for nine years, is the same.

I was in my small London apartment and I had no milk. I wanted a coffee. It was night-time, and late. I went out my apartment door, down the stairs and straight out on to the street. Closing the door behind me, I was instantly struck by the bright lights, buzz, and energy. I was in Times Square, New York. Off I went in search of milk and never questioned the shopkeeper happily accepting my pound coins instead of dollars. I got my milk, walked under the neon lights, got to my apartment, made my coffee, sat down to watch the BBC News. Although London is a busy city, the apartment always felt silent and peaceful.

When I woke up, I was not in London or New York, I was in my bed in Dublin.

Dreams can be incredibly powerful and memorable and it takes a little time to wake up and realise that a dream is not reality. Our minds can trick us, and it is hard to argue with yourself.

And though danger is real, fear is not. Try telling your mind that when it has you in its grip.

If a dream can be as illogical and yet real as this, then that is an effective way to understand just how real fear is for most of us.

My Nervous Friend

I have known Paul a long time, but I do not know him well. He is a gentle soul but always afraid. He lives in perpetual fear. A tough card to be dealt. Like many men, he would rather suffer a minor ailment than go to the doctor. This time, his health problem was not going away, nothing was working. He needed to get past his fear and get checked out. Eventually, he did.

At last, he would get fixed and some certainty, or so I thought.

Shortly after his appointment, we met. I was expecting a refreshed and content soul. Instead, approaching him, it was easy to spot his depressed posture. I was worried. Worried that his minor ailment was no longer minor. I lightened the mood as best I could, and it wasn't long before my "How are you?" taught me a powerful lesson.

"I'm fine, I think", came an intuitive reply.

Should I dig deeper or let it go?

I dug deeper. "What do you mean 'I think'?"

Paul explained that his doctor was very upbeat, not at all concerned and said he would be right as rain in a few days.

Confused, I asked him what was there to think about. It transpired that as Paul left the doctor's office, he wanted the fastest exit possible. As he hotfooted by Reception, he was met with a cold, "Hello, Paul. Hello.

Can you come back, please? We need to book another appointment for you".

This was news to Paul and not good news. The doctor had told him everything was fine, but this did not match that message. Getting scared, Paul mustered up the courage to ask the detached receptionist why he needed to come back. In a slightly bored voice, she responded nonchalantly, "Oh, it could be something and nothing".

His appointment was four weeks away. He suffered. He Googled the phrase. We discussed it many times. It was eating him alive.

Four tortuous weeks passed slowly. He almost did not go, but he did. Again, the doctor was cheerful, upbeat, and positive. His opening words?

"You seemed very nervous on your last visit, Paul. I was keen to check in with you to see how you're doing. So how are you?"

'Something and nothing' are exactly that. Something that says nothing. And what does that mean? It means exactly what George Bernard Shaw said.

Game Playing

Game playing, especially at work, is the pursuit of power regardless of the damage inflicted along the way. Game players may be in positions of power but that never justifies the act. Inevitably, time exposes them, and their cruelty is long remembered. I know, it happened to me.

Game playing is insecurity but that does not always involve people; it involves deceit.

An Early Monday Meeting

In the mid 1980s, the 'Troubles' in Northern Ireland were at their dreadful height. People were dying in the most traumatic way. Fear festered in every corner. It was a dark place on the brightest day.

Mainland UK was not immune, and some shocking atrocities were visited on ordinary people. A civilised innocent society was poisoned by the overflowing anger of a tribal war.

It was no surprise that some people tarnished every Irish citizen with the label 'terrorist'.

My boss was very British, right down to the turned-up trousers and Union Jack cufflinks accentuating his Yorkshire wool suit.

He disliked Irish people and I had been imposed on him by his boss. He did not like that either.

I was never "Conor"; always either "Irish" or "Kenny". It was an overt indicator of what was to come.

Central London, where I lived, looks great to a visitor or tourist. For a young man, it is bleak and lonely. The majority of people who come into London to work disappear the same day. It is like the tide rushing in and slipping back out. Saturdays and Sundays were always quiet.

We always had a meeting at 9:00 am on a Monday. It was routine and Jerry, my boss, lived a long way from London, and it took him over two hours each way, every day. Nothing was going to happen before 9:00, ever.

I was doing OK. Nothing great, but nothing bad either. In sales, we were highly measurable. Others were doing far worse.

Late afternoon one Friday, I could see Jerry preparing for an early exit. He was not in good form. He swivelled this way and that, like a radar trying to find something threatening to attack. I could see he decided to intercept me. He took off from his superior status chair and headed straight for my desk.

Leaning in front of me, arms sprawling on my desk, he looked me in the eye and in a voice straight out of *The Godfather* movie he said, "I want to see you here, alone, at 8:00 am on Monday".

I was afraid.

I was coming up to my six-month probation and could not afford to lose my job. I was afraid.

That weekend was destroyed and left a scar. I was restless, unsettled, worried, fearful, and unable to do anything other than submit to the paralysis of fear.

No matter what was going to happen, I just needed it to be over. The pain was unbearable.

Monday came and, after a bad night's sleep, I was in the office at 7:45 am. I was fuelling my own fear very successfully.

At 8.00 am, I was breathing deeply to control the anxiety. No Jerry yet.

21

At 8:30 am, I was close to exhaustion. No Jerry.

9:00 am. Still no Jerry.

At 9:15 am, in came Jerry in unusually good form. I watched and waited. He was very late for our 8:00 am meeting. I waited, watched, and waited. Nothing showed his desire to meet.

At 9.30 am, I could not contain myself any longer. I went to his desk and I was greeted by an exceedingly rare smile.

"Yes, Kenny. What can I do for you?"

"We were to meet at 8.00 am today, Jerry".

He looked a little confused, paused and said, "Were we? What for?".

In my mind, I could hear the steely click of my shotgun loading.

In French, please

When I was 15, I did what many students of my age did then. I did a student swap to France.

My French was awful, but I was not unduly worried because everyone spoke some English, so I would get by.

Your destination, the family you would be with, was a complete lottery. I was nervous. In Lyon, in the heart of France, I was still waiting patiently for my new family to collect me from the airport. Soon, there were just five of us waiting to be collected. Then four, three, two and, finally, just me.

I have a tiny amount of money. I speak almost no French. I am sitting on a suitcase in a foreign land and I am paralysed with it all. I wait and wait and wait. All sorts of wild scenarios start to play in my imagination. It would happen to me, wouldn't it?

Eventually the family arrived. By then, I was a confused, emotional wreck. Then an exceptionally large spoonful of salt was thrown onto a vicious open wound. They spoke no English. None. Not a word. Not "Yes", not "No". Nothing.

I sat in the car in silence. We simply could not communicate, other than the dad doing his best to believe I suddenly had perfect French and could understand his rambling descriptions of this and that. I retreated into my 15-year-old world.

Six weeks later, I appeared with French so fluent that a French girl asked me what part of France I was from. I treasured that moment boastfully for many years. This was one way to learn. If you want to eat, learn. If you want to ring home, learn. If you want to exist, then learn. It was tough but the payoff was spectacular.

Some 16 years later, in London, there was a dreadful recession. Simply, there were no jobs, but I was not going to roll over and die. I could not. This was survival.

I saw an advert for a sales job of some description. Part of the fundamental requirement was fluent French. I applied and I got a fast response inviting me for a first telephone interview. My hopes were high.

The due date arrived, and I was back guarding my favourite red telephone box and armed with every coin I could muster from an ever-decreasing pot. On the button, I called and got straight through. A lovely woman told me she would be doing the interview. I was feeling confident and I had my story rehearsed. Then, she said we would be holding the conversation all in French. I froze. I was not expecting this.

Even though 16 years had passed since I was taken for being authentic, I was convinced my basic command of the language would be better than most. She started with a quite simple question. I knew the answer. In my head, I could relay this perfectly in French, but my mouth would not work. She was incredibly patient. Fear was poisoning my body. She asked another question and all she ever heard was "Ummm, ahhh, errr". I was like a motorbike that just could not be kicked into life. The paralysis was moving towards my knees and toes. It was a dreadful situation. She tried again and after another attempt, over maybe seven or eight minutes, I was incapable of giving her even one word in French. It was like waiting for the Roman Emperor to give the inevitable thumbs down and all I needed next was to be dinner for the lions.

With dignity and kindness, she reverted to speaking English, thanked me for my time and released me from the phone box from hell. I pushed the door and almost fell out on to the street in shock. I could not understand how it had gone so wrong, but it taught me several precious lessons.

If you are trying to communicate in fear, the chances are it will get worse. It taught me to assume less and know more. Lastly, it taught me that there are a lot of kind, patient people who will listen with care to what you say. If they have to say "No" to us, they cannot be blamed; it is up to us to be ready, researched, prepared and never to wing it in the belief that we are good enough.

We all live with fear in varying degrees and we fear different things. It is a part of being human and all fear is simply excessive non-existential imagination. Fear is a trick of the mind because we can never conquer or defeat that which is not real, that which does not exist. We can cope with what is real, what does exist and the quickest way out of fear is straight through. Freedom will always lie on the far side of fear and we cannot reach anything if we allow it to have its imaginary way.

> *He who does not succeed in taking his anxiety courageously upon himself can succeed in avoiding the extreme situation of despair by escaping into neurosis. He still affirms himself but on a limited scale. Neurosis is the way of avoiding nonbeing by avoiding being.*
>
> ### *Paul Tillich,* **The Courage to Be**

4: THE BULLY

A bully is playing a game, one that he or she enjoys and needs.
You're welcome to play this game if it makes you happy, but for
most people, it will make you miserable.

Seth Godin

If we bully somebody, we are trying to punish them. Bullying reflects a flagging ego that is in constant search of fuel to prop itself up. Like a greedy thirst, it cannot be satisfied and, eventually, the bully's antics will not be tolerated. Their goal is power, control and to be somebody. It is a path that can never lead to success, happiness, or a legacy to be proud of.

Bullies are dangerous people. Their self-obsession leaves no room to consider their impact – which can be devastating.

In people, it is wrong.

In business, it is the end of a brand.

Not long ago, a wonderful young girl wrote to me just after losing her job. I knew her; the company made a bad mistake. Her story annoyed me and, in all of 90 seconds, I wrote the following short post for my LinkedIn page. I have authored articles, blogs and short posts for LinkedIn for over 11 years – but this post was read over 6,000 times in five days.

I Was Thrown Out

A young professional did not lose her job when the pandemic hit.

In her words, "I was thrown out the door".

We knew her because we had trained her. She stood out because her deep concentration, smart questions, and her desire to consume as much knowledge as possible was heart-warming.

Her former company's marketing is particularly good, clever, engaging and well-positioned. It tells a story and creates an aura of a wonderful place to work but ... she was thrown out.

And they forgot something.

The interaction and experience we have of your brand are often with the most junior and those on the lowest wage. They are your brand and, often, we really like them.

But if you do not treat them properly, invest in their future, respect their loyalty and low-paid demanding work then, in time, guess who will be thrown out?

Think before you throw anyone out and put your juniors first.

Better still, put them on a pedestal and say, "Thank you".

What does that tell you?

That we, the world, do not like bullies.

Bad Boys

We, the world, do not like bullies.

In business, sometimes we meet people who bully their staff and some who bully their customers.

Bullying is intrinsically linked to arrogance but never confuse arrogance with confidence. For me, confidence is supported by substance, but arrogance has none.

Arrogance is often because someone is wrong, but they just cannot climb down.

In another person, arrogance occurs because you are, in fact, right but the listener cannot accept it.

We have all met them. Here are two of my most memorable meetings.

The Man Who Bullied His Staff

He did not walk, he swaggered. His most common phrase was "I don't care". He was young and he had power. It went to his head and nothing is more irritating than a young man who has just discovered something and thinks it was his idea.

He had a young team, who were still in that early career phase where we all try to fit in, do our work, understand the dynamics, and balance it all at once. Not easy for a young fresh mind.

Worse still if the honesty is deliberately confused by a bully with an agenda. That agenda was control.

They were eager and humble, and a class was about to begin. Excitement filled the room. I was looking forward to fuelling that energy even further.

But no sign of the arrogant young man.

We settled and were about to start what we had come into the room to do.

The door burst open and in came the gunslinger. I am sure he waited for this perfect moment and imagined him ear to the door awaiting this perfect moment.

This was his moment, and, like a drunk peacock, he swaggered aimlessly around the exceptionally large room.

Then he spoke.

First, he offloaded the essential clichés about this and that but it was only time before he finished on a different note.

The superficial talk was ending. The face darkening, the eyes closing.

"If any of you mess about, don't pay attention or try to be disruptive then you'll find yourselves in my office and there'll be consequences. (Pause) Grave consequences."

With that, he was gone.

It was difficult to understand how anyone could have seen anything other than enthusiasm, a thirst for knowledge and good humour – but this was his way.

At lunchtime, he miraculously appeared again precisely as we took our break. Lunch was a buffet nearby and it felt like we were corralled into a carefully disguised pen that could be easily seen.

He strutted some more. This time, he threw the occasional meaningless, self-serving scrap. The words were neutral clichés but what was far more interesting was the nervous laughter, the shuffle to avoid, the darting eyes.

This man created fear and then revelled in the egoist short thrill that followed.

I was furious but it was not for me to raise the stakes.

Like a politician at election time, he waded uninvited into every conversation. More asserting his power.

I had enough and was about to sound the signal that it was time to go back to work.

Just then, he set his sights on me and I almost wanted a row.

This time, he was uneasy, the voice softer. I knew he was preparing for something.

Leaning in, careful not to be overheard, he said, "What do they think of me?"

I looked him in the eye and said, "They think you're a bully".

He was stunned, wounded, and surprised. He drifted backwards slowly, still staring. I stood still and I stared back. Not threatening, simply reinforcing that it was a real comment.

He walked a slow, wide, stunned circle right around until he was back facing me again.

"Do they really think that? Do they really think I'm a bully?"

I paused and said, "Yes. The answer remains the same".

A tiny light dawned. That afternoon, he joined in. He was engaging, he was charming, and he was humble.

The young people loved it. I did not.

As I left that night, I could not help but think that it was only time before the demon ego would take hold and it would start all over again.

The Online Bully

Being in service or of service means to serve.

That jars with some people who have chosen this career.

They like the role, status and fun but they never want to feel subservient.

I met one such man socially and he gleefully recounted this story.

He despised his customers, and, in his own way, he was going to let them know.

They were the enemy. Subtlety was not his strong point.

He ran an exceptionally fine boutique townhouse where I was staying in a beautiful rural part of the UK.

The detail and comfort were something to be proud of and the food was heavenly. But he despised customers.

His best bedroom looked out on a field, a working field full of the hustle and rush of farming life. Given its rural location, peace and fresh air were two beautiful bonuses to a normal, anonymous, high street stay.

A young couple came to stay, and they were not happy. Unfairly, they took to a review site to share their disappointment.

Four things really upset them:

- First, there was no air-conditioning on a hot summer's night;
- Second, the cows woke them early as they began their grazing day;
- Third, a tractor came too close to their window and they felt that disturbed their rest too;
- Last, they took their anger out on the 'manager' who seemed indifferent, and suggested the owner might consider "getting rid of him".

The owner was furious and, in a moment of temper, he committed his thoughts to an online reply.

It went something like this.

Dear Young Couple,
I'm sure you don't get to stay in guest houses or hotels very often so let me explain a few things to you.
This is England, rural England. You may well have noticed fields full of animals as you drove here.
England lies north of the equator and sadly, we do not often enjoy hot summers that merit air-conditioning. Instead, we open our windows and we find that perfectly adequate.
I am so deeply sorry the cows had to be moved. If you come again, I will see if we can arrange for you, or the cows, to move at the precise moment you would prefer.
As for the tractor, again I am sorry this standard piece of farm equipment, dating back to the first tractor Mr. Dan Albone built in 1901 (more details on request), bothered you. I know Mr. Harry Ferguson's version of 1917 was regarded as quieter and more popular. However, to

recognise your upset, myself and my wife are going to buy the first all-electric tractor as soon as it is available.

I must also apologise most sincerely regarding your last point.

I brought your review to the attention of my present wife, Betty, who served your breakfast, and she asked me to reply to say she agrees with you fully but after 30 years of trying, she has given up.

With best wishes,

John, Farmer, Cook, Housekeeper, Bar Tender, Stock Controller and Online Review Manager

Ouch!

5: WHAT'S MOTIVATING YOU

My motivation to write is because I like to teach people the lessons I have learnt. Teachers, a little like frontline medical and healthcare professionals, are the most dedicated people with the least visibility. They blend in and rarely do they ever look for or get the spotlight.

But think about it if you were sick, whose words offer comfort, hope, and joy? If you were struggling at school, who had the patience to understand, explain and help you move on? What they have in common is that their words have a lot of power. We remember teachers who exploded, had favourites, and humiliated some students. We remember our fears being calmed when we were sick. Both understand what we mean by impact.

In my career, I have been fired, made redundant and not paid for work I did. Whilst they are not pleasant events, they teach you more than the event itself.

In London, being unemployed and without enough money to pay for anything, I came away with powerful lessons that changed me. Sometimes, we need to experience things to understand them. Sometimes, for example, having nothing allows you understand the dreadful peril of homeless people. Later in life, we go full circle and go back to these things but, this time, armed with wisdom, experience and knowing the way out.

That is what teaching is, showing someone the way, a way.

That is why I love to teach and that love is underpinned by two notions:

- First, my own desire to be understood;
- Second, to share my many mistakes with younger people in business to help them avoid tumbling unnecessarily into the same potholes.

The deeper and more meaningful question to ask is not what motivates you but to understand where that motivation has its origins.

If we understand that, we can also understand that it is an eternal flame that drives us – one that cannot be easily extinguished.

In communicating with people, this is the most potent accelerant and if we understand it, we understand ourselves.

The Bravest Man

In my last book, *It's Who I Am*, I went on a crusade to talk in depth to 14 extraordinarily successful people. I wanted to understand where their motivation came from and what drove them. Curiously, as soon as you say 'extraordinarily successful people', there is a default thought to fame, fortune, and a limousine lifestyle. That is shallow.

Success is relative. Success, for me, means achieving what it is you set out to achieve. Although there are well-known famous faces in the book, some of the best stories came from those beneath the radar and I really wanted to hear their story.

When they talk, the influences appear and inevitably they are in childhood. For example, Lieutenant Commander Roberta O'Brien, the first woman to command an Irish Navy battleship and, as this book went to print, the Irish Navy's first woman to be appointed Commander, who captained the local boys Gaelic football team. It was such a gorgeous insight into an incredible career because it never crossed her mind that she would not captain a boy's football team.

Be who you are and say what you feel, because those who mind don't matter, and those who matter don't mind.

Bernard M. Baruch

All their stories had memorable moments but, for me, one story stood out head and shoulders.

Paul Kimmage is one of Ireland's most engaging writers. The greatest sports people in the world have bared their souls to him and he has a gift for drawing out the true story, probing with interest, efficiency, and empathy.

He writes beautifully.

I did not know Paul, but I wanted to. There is a fearlessness in what he does, and it underlies his work.

And you might ask where that comes from. It comes from an upbringing in a very tight-knit family and an early love of cycling that took him to the very top of this brutal sport. He was driven, and immersed in sport and family and especially his comrade in arms, his late brother Raphael. They were cut from the one cloth.

I have gotten to know Paul over the last few years, and I come away from every coffee feeling enlightened. His gift of intense listening would make anyone feel good. Like all achievers, he is humble, understated and enormously respectful of the company he is in.

When I sat with Paul to do his interview for the book, I was doing my absolute best to at least look intelligent because here I was turning the hose on one of the greatest interviewers of his time. Somehow, this man had accepted this invitation into the unknown.

My first question was "What are you?"

When I asked the same question to the others in the book, some answers were instant, some well-rehearsed, a few natural, some thought-provoking and then came Paul's answer.

Raising his eyes slowly from the floor, he said, "I'm afraid".

This was real. It was natural and, as I was to discover, Paul being Paul and that means honest.

I felt the hair standing on the back of my neck. I made sure I stayed silent and, in time, the most wonderful story appeared. It was like listening to the best movie you could not see.

Paul is often accused of being negative because he has pursued drug-free sports all his life. Paul is not afraid. He relentlessly challenges those who have no respect for the level playing field and seek a laboratory-manufactured advantage.

If you enjoy superficial judgement, then a superficial analysis could report Paul as being grumpy. He is not. He is happy and far from grumpy.

Paul is in search of the truth. Nothing more. If that means challenging questions to people surrounded by PR specialists and spin doctors, Paul is going to do it. He does it because cheating is wrong. If he gets a whiff of it, he will chase it down relentlessly.

Paul is the embodiment of Mark Twain's quote:

If you tell the truth, you don't have to remember anything.

Often, doing the right thing will be far more difficult than the easy thing.

That means stepping out of our comfort zone.

Now, I understand why Paul said he was afraid.

Come to think of it, isn't that what we all should be if we are to turn our dreams into achievable goals?

You see, where our motivation originates is the fuel for our purpose. What if Paul Kimmage was never beaten in a race by someone who was not playing on a level pitch?

When you look deeper, you see where our purpose comes from.

If you understand your motivation and your purpose, then it is worth investing a little time to understand the opposite view too.

Isn't that how the whole picture emerges?

Jonathan Went Mad

Some years back, I was mentoring an exceptionally fine young man.

He studied hard, worked hard and, in a remarkably successful sporting life, he trained hard.

Every time we met, he was early, prepared and perfectly dressed. He impressed in every way.

One day, I got a call from Jonathan. He was agitated and his normal fluent style was not happening. He rambled, agitated. After a little time, I asked him what was bugging him. He said, "There's a manager in my office and he's bullying a young girl".

I listened some more, and I could hear the volcano gurgling. It was time to let him let off steam. The story went on.

In the end, I said, "You can't intervene in every battle and this is a battle you can't win. For now, just try to park this. I will be near your office in a few days. Come have coffee".

We met and he was calm. The first thing I said to him was "Tell me about growing up in this town".

It lit a fuse. I sat back waiting to see what it was that drove this fine man. It did not take long.

He adored his mother. She was an integral part of every story. After a scenic journey through his early life, one thing struck me. He never once mentioned his father. It was thin ice, but I needed to understand how this passion could be understood so it would not overturn him. As gently as I could, I asked about the rest of his family. He said it was just him and his Mum. Then silence. I did not break it.

Lifting his head slowly, he started to tell me all about his Dad. It was not a good or happy story. It was a story full of addiction and violence. His father ended up in prison.

You see, every time Jonathan saw a bully, saw a row, saw violence, it triggered a nightmare memory. He was re-living an unhappy childhood, helpless to protect his adored Mum at the hands of his dysfunctional Dad.

As soon as he realised this and what power it had, he understood himself far better.

I remember telling him that to understand your motivation is amazing but to know what that means is even better. He asked me what I meant. I told him that, in the right hands, a sharp carving knife can do a wonderful job. In the wrong hands or not used properly, it can quickly become a lethal weapon. The knife is always neutral. How we apply it is up to us.

Today, Jonathan is a tremendous success in his chosen career, and we stay in touch. More importantly, he understands why he minds his Mum so well even if she keeps telling him not to spoil her. She always adds a wink and a smile to that statement.

6: PROMISES

*A "No" does not hide anything, but a "Yes" very easily becomes
a deception.*

Soren Kierkegaard

If you think about it, all communication holds an element of promise:

- "See you at 7";
- "No need to worry";
- "I'll look after it";
- "Trust me".

Promises flow easily and, often, people do not really realise what they are promising or, more importantly, the impact of that promise on the other person.

We make promises to predict a stable future so that we can instil a certain reliability. It is a curious concept because that is one thing we will never be able to do – to control the future.

Promises are powerful words. They are based on trust (more on that shortly). Promises were never meant to be broken and whoever coined that phrase may as well have said all criminal behaviour is entirely justified. Rubbish: promises are meant to be kept – that is the very essence of a promise.

Promises create hope – often against a bad or sad background. If you break a promise, you break trust and that has its own outcome.

Promises are overlaid with emotion and what we say as a promise will be believed, at least until you prove them wrong.

Delivered promises leave an impression. They become a label of admiration, but we rarely remember the detail of the promise, just the sentiment and sense of the person.

Think of your friendly painter; he always showed up on time. Think of your parents collecting you from a train station; they were there. Think of your best friend and the times you needed their shoulder; they were there too.

Broken promises are different. We remember the specifics, the detail, the betrayal, the person, where, when and how.

If we considered the impact of a broken promise before we indulged ourselves in the glory of making one, we would tread slowly.

You see, if there is a deep private emotion relieved by the wonderful promise you make, then I will be happy because of it. If you make me a promise that steps on my emotional toes, then I will never forget.

You have heard it before, but this simple wisdom is a wonderful compass.

Don't promise when you are happy, don't reply when you are angry, and don't decide when you are sad.

Unknown

See You at 8

Up by Iron River in north Wisconsin, USA, I found myself a quiet corner daydreaming in a little rowing boat on a peaceful lake. Overhead, a golden eagle surveyed all below and, in hindsight, even me.

Back before digital everything, a photo took days to get developed, sometimes weeks. After the holiday, I studiously left my film in to be developed. No instant image then but it was fun to wonder how the pictures turned out. Sometimes, you would get a wonderful surprise of a captured moment; sometimes, a shock.

I got the latter.

Lying on the little boat, someone noticed I had drifted into a deep sleep. My photo was taken. I did not know. Like everyone else, I raced through the freshly-developed photos and to my horror, there I was, asleep and looking more like a small buffalo rather than my self-image of an 'average' shape.

It had such an impact that I decided to join a gym the next day.

I did. This is what happened.

Over the next 24 hours, my self-confidence declined. I flipped from denial to blaming the camera, and from the camera to acceptance and back again. It was horrible. One photo had delivered so much turmoil.

I made my way to the local big gym. In the car, the battle of the devil and angel began.

"Stay, Conor. You are in great shape."

"No, you are not, Conor. Deny all you like and be the buffalo. Your choice."

I chose the angel.

In I went, trying my best to look like this was normal. I did not want to be the newbie.

Up to the desk and that inevitable "How can I help you?". Feigning a slightly impartial persona, I said I would like to chat to someone about joining.

In minutes, I was in their clever enrolling system. In came Susan, bouncing. Her smile was a bright spot on an insecure night.

I did my best to give the impression I knew everything, with serious nodding and concentration. Inside, I had no idea what 75% of the jargon meant.

The promises were free-flowing and in a matter of weeks, if not days, I would have the body of a Greek god, a circle of friends, live forever and have a social diary that would neatly require all this extra energy I was destined to have.

I bought the message. I was hooked.

"Now, Conor. When would you like to start working out?".

Filled with some in-built ecstasy, I said that tomorrow night would be perfect.

"Perfect, simply perfect. Say 8:00 pm? I'll be here and I'll meet you and show you around."

I went home feeling fantastic.

At the appointed hour, I was there. In fact, I was there 20 minutes early, like a young boy starting a new school. With three minutes to go, a horrible thought invaded the last of my leaky confidence. Was I dressed the right way? Did my gym clothes match the style of the place? Fear started to rule but I pushed through, just.

Regaining my slightly detached persona, I swaggered up to the desk and told them I was here to meet Susan. The man behind the desk looked at me and said, "Susan?".

I confirmed it was Susan.

"Susan in sales?", he probed further.

Again, I confirmed it was this very Susan.

"Hmmm" came the slow reply. "There must be some misunderstanding. Susan only works until lunchtime, Monday to Friday. I'm afraid you must be confusing her with someone else."

I was not and over 20 years later, I am telling you this story.

Broken promises leave lasting memories.

At the point that our promises have become tactics to get what we want verses commitments that we intend to keep, the only thing that we are promising is the delivery of a broken promise.

Craig D. Lounsbrough

7: TRUST ME

Trust is fundamental to any relationship. Without trust, there is nothing but the silent preparation of sound defences. Trust is the glue in every relationship and the bedrock of integrity.

In life, in business, we are destined to meet many people we cannot trust. But everyone you meet who deceives you, steals from you or mistreats you, does you a favour. Each unpleasant interaction with well-camouflaged thieves, pretenders, scavengers, and nasty people teaches us powerful and memorable lessons. Of course, it is inevitable that we will continue to be conned, mistreated, and taken advantage of but that is never our fault, it is theirs. The right thing can never be wrong simply because the other person saw an opportunity. And, in the words of Winston Churchill:

We will remember them.

Trust equals integrity. Integrity is woven over many years and comes from a desire to do the right thing. It is a moral compass and not one that is always easy to adhere to. To be trusted is a wonderful compliment.

If you are not trusted, that is a dreadful reflection on where you are.

Naturally, we get it wrong both ways from time to time.

No matter how eloquent, articulate, and polished, if there is no trust, you will simply be showboating, and so your content will never be heard.

Beware the Man who says Trust Me

Many years ago, I lived on Kings Road in London. It was the ultimate street to people-watch. One Sunday morning, I joined the great, good and famous and sat alone in a very ordinary café drinking coffee. In line with my earlier Jean Paul Sartre story about role play, I found myself falling temporarily into this trap and adopting the persona of a long-time rich Kings Road resident.

Surrounding Kings Road are some of London's most expensive houses, populated by the very wealthy. Though I had no idea who was who, it was fun to wonder. I decided on a second coffee, a serious decision for someone so terribly broke. And, I thought, if I am going to have a second coffee, then I had better fall in and read a paper. Off I went next door and, I think, for the first time in my life I bought *The Sunday Times*. Sitting down again in the café, I was determined to look like this was what I always did on a Sunday. The reality was two coffees and one newspaper had consumed a third of my remaining money for the week ahead.

In hindsight, it was worth it.

Having spent a pretty penny on these upper-class indulgences, I was determined to read the paper. I did.

On the second page was a full-page article. Its title was 'Beware the Man Who Says Trust Me'.

It was a simple heading and the story went on to make one simple point. That is, people you trust never say "Trust me".

To this day, when someone says that, I can hear the drawbridge being hauled up to the sound of loud urgent alarm bells.

The Man Who Took Me to Lunch

We start out in life a little too innocent and naive. We trust everyone. When we make the next big jump and go out into the vast ocean of starting a business, we are just as green. I certainly was.

For there to be betrayal, there would have to have been trust first.

Suzanne Collins

Like most people, I relied too much on intuition and instinct. In later life, that wrong balance changed to intuition and record of accomplishment. The art and the science.

He was a well-known businessperson in the centre of the city and his business was doing very well. What a catch. A well-known businessperson with a successful business. We met several times in his luxurious premises. His briefings for the programme were detailed and he wanted me to help develop their management skills. We agreed the contract and away we went. Halfway through, he showed great interest, was lavish in his praise from what he was hearing from the course participants and then he took me to lunch. I was enjoying every aspect of this assignment. I was where I wanted to be. The programme finished. They considered it to be a success; their written feedback confirmed as much.

And then.

He had suggested the 20% deposit. I gladly accepted the cheque. And then I could not get paid the outstanding 80%. Despite my best efforts, nothing happened.

Over time, I had no choice but to sue him. At last, he responded. I was optimistic that it was some innocent mistake. I was wrong. He denied that he had ever met me, even though his CCTV system could show me meeting him. He denied I gave workshops, but they were on camera too. He denied he had ever commissioned me, but I had his emails. He denied there was ever any financial interaction, but I had a photocopy of his cheque. We went to court and he stuck to his guns. We won the case, but we never got paid. A year later, I walked by his premises. The company had gone out of business and he would have denied that too.

You see, we all get over these things, we move on, but the imprint is filed away. All these years later, it is easy to reach into the filing cabinet of our mind and pluck out the paperwork. Trust is only ever one lie away from being over. If I cannot trust you, there is no communication in the world that will ever polish away hard learnt lessons.

If I do not trust you, if I cannot believe you, our conversation may take place, but it is no more valuable than the drunk man having a heated debate with a statue. When he comes around, there will be no more to say.

And a simple and useful guiding light for all of us?

If you tell the truth, you don't have to remember anything.

Mark Twain

8: IMPACT

If you have ever managed to sit in or even peer into the studio of a large radio broadcasting company, then you will be instantly struck by how small and intimate it is. Besides the two people – the presenter and the interviewee – there is just a table and some technology.

With you and a well-known iconic broadcaster, it is difficult to believe hundreds of thousands are out there in the unseen world listening. But they are.

Reality is often what we see, not what we know.

When the broadcaster transmits, just like someone throwing a stone over a high wall, we see its departure, but we do not see where it lands. Or its impact.

How we communicate is a little like that.

The question is simple: What impact are you making?

We must never underestimate the impact we make, regardless of where we stand. There is always an impact, good and bad, and that impact has a strong ripple effect long after the words are uttered.

Bad Words

Words can hurt and heal, build, and destroy.

One day a friend of mine said, "Words are just words, they're harmless".

We nearly fell out over it yet, in hindsight, that had more to do with his exceptional self-confidence rather than a disregard for anyone. Still, I would not let go. Later that night, I wrote to him unhappy that I had not convinced him.

I asked him to reply with an honest fast emotion if any of the following were said to him:

- "I'm afraid you've lost your house";
- "You got the job";
- "You're fired";
- "You won the jackpot";
- "Your holiday is cancelled";
- "You've just been asked on to the board of a big company";
- "He is going to sue you";
- "You're very sick I'm sorry to say".

Here are his answers:

- "I'm afraid you've lost your house" – "I won't accept that. I'll deal with it";
- "You got the job" – "Nice";
- "You're fired" – "Wouldn't bother me as long as they pay me off";
- "You won the jackpot" – "How much?";
- "Your holiday is cancelled" – "I'll book another";
- "You've just been asked on to the board of a big company" – "Cool";
- "He is going to sue you" – "Bring it on";
- "You're extremely sick I'm sorry to say" – "Oh, how sick? Are you serious?".

What does this tell you? It gives you a clear insight into the DNA of the man. You can sense what bothers him, what does not. What excites him, what does not. What moves him to action, what does not.

But this is all of us. If you asked 100 people for their responses to these statements, you would get 100 different answers.

That is what makes us who we are and a simple example of what bothers or excites you will be the opposite of what affects me.

Choosing your words carefully is a clever idea. Remember the saying:

Never put in writing what you wouldn't want to read in the newspaper.

An Early Boss

It is easy to throw away a remark like "He's arrogant" and I was guilty until I dived a little deeper. Arrogance is a superior attitude without substance. Confidence is based on substance and may appear arrogant. There is a difference.

One of my very first managers was both arrogant and confident. He was a high achiever – and still is. Even though I have seen his superb career from afar, it only ever reminds me of one tiny event that happened a long time ago.

He was a busy man and always in a hurry. He walked fast and had little time for idle chat or long-winded messages. He created fear easily, deliberate or not.

I needed to speak to him about something and saw him gliding down the exceptionally long corridor of the old building. I made haste and almost ran to catch up with him. With a gap of about five metres, I called out his name, "Dan. May I have a brief word?".

I could almost imagine squealing tyres and a puff of smoke he stopped so hard. He stood still, deathly still. I froze. No speed now.

He turned slowly, very slowly and with a piercing look and in a low tone, he said, "Daniel, not Dan. Daniel".

Then he was gone.

Although my initial response was emotionally driven, this was a potent early lesson that trying to succeed in business would fail if every interaction was going to be taken personally.

Nice Shirts

There was a recession and I could not get a job. Money was running out fast, with the dangerous consequences that come with it.

I got an interview with a very posh company and to my astonishment, I got the job. It paid well, rewarded performance very well and it came with a very fancy company car.

I was determined to make a success of this excellent opportunity.

Everyone looked so successful – clearly the reward for demanding work and a very profitable company. The managing director was the most beautifully dressed man ever.

I was instantly self-conscious of my cheap suit and lack of options.

One month into the job and still without my first salary cheque, I was at zero on every front. I had already spent my wages in my head, and, in time, I would be able to buy new clothes, just not yet.

My best shirt was a plain light pink shirt. I had always found ironing difficult. It could take me an hour to do one shirt.

I always wanted to make the absolute best of my work clothes. I went in the next day thinking I was dressed well in my best shirt, tie and slightly worn suit. It gives you a whiff of confidence.

Around noon, as I was walking close to the managing director's office, he was coming towards me. The confidence was still high. He said, "Good morning" and carried on without more. In seconds, that changed.

"Kenny, come here".

I went, wondering what he could want.

"Kenny, would you ever go buy yourself some proper shirts and make an effort to dress better?"

Then he was gone. I could have wept.

And the legacy of a 10 second remark? To this day, I have a wardrobe full of brand-new shirts – just in case.

Gerry, the Criminal Lawyer

School, in my day, did not have anything like the political correctness that today's youth enjoy. Words and deeds could be brutal, and the culture of that time was insensitive to impressionable, growing young minds.

Teachers were all powerful and capable of incredible kindness – and also the very opposite. They ruled the room, for better for worse, and sensitive language was not easy for some.

Gerry, like me, was a middle of the road student. Nothing much stood out. We were not high achievers in any arena.

Like all students, we have subjects we are good at and subjects that are not easy. Maths was my Achilles heel and it was Gerry's too. The teacher could humiliate with ease and revelled in the nervous compliant laughter of his regular public hangings.

I got off lightly when my turn came, but Gerry did not.

In a vicious tantrum, the teacher told Gerry that there was little point in him doing the final two years in school because he was so stupid. He was told to go home and tell his parents that he should stop wasting their money and would they please place him in a tradesman's job as soon as possible.

Fast forward 20 years.

I had often considered a career in law at the Bar, but I did not have the appetite to study hard. Court fascinated me, especially the criminal court. I was fascinated by the defence and prosecution. The victim and the person in the dock. The strategies, arguments, and outcomes. It was live theatre and it was very real. It was exciting and frightening, interesting and, most of all, an incredible look at life through a vastly different lens.

There had been an infamous murder wrapped up with every subtext you can imagine. It was big news and the wigs and gowns added to the drama.

I was not going to miss out and, for days, I took up my right to sit in the public gallery and watch the story unfold. A thriller that would conclude right before my eyes.

On day one, the central public area was buzzing with life. Gowns took off like wings and wigs fell to the floor, such was the urgency.

As I loitered watching all of this, I felt a huge punch on my back. The boxer was wearing a wig and gown and I did not know who it was. He took off his wig and said, "It's Gerry".

I was taken aback but really pleased to see him all these years later. He asked me what I was doing there, and I told him I wanted to watch this infamous trial that was a global story then. He smiled and said, "I'd better do an excellent job then".

I asked him what he meant.

"I'm defending the accused."

Not bad for someone told to leave school early.

But impact can be good, and it too can leave a powerful print.

Norman Davey

This book is dedicated to Norman.

With two years to go before I finished secondary school, I was despatched to boarding school in the midlands.

For a boy of 15, it was no different to being exiled to the most remote corner of the earth. I hated it.

Mount St. Joseph's Abbey near Roscrea, Tipperary, is a place of beauty, tranquillity, and prayer. Run by the Cistercian monks, the boarding school thrives to this day and its alumni have reached the highest offices in the land in sport, politics, and business.

At 15, none of that had any impact.

Today, it does, enormously.

When I look back at the kindness, devotion and lessons learnt, it was the best thing that could have happened to me. Its impact and legacy have an exceedingly long life. Today, my best friend from Mount St. Joseph's, Vincent and I can see the values that were taught to us.

I was not a gifted academic nor did I want to be.

This is not the heroic story of an average student who went on to excel in the Olympics. I was average at that too.

This is a story about impact, not prowess.

I had a teacher, Norman Davey. Like me, he was from Dublin so I felt a little bond.

On mid-term breaks, Norman would pile three or four of the few Dublin students into his tiny Triumph Herald car and bring us to the capital. It was a contradiction, escaping with a teacher.

Norman taught French and students loved him. I found it difficult, and I was certainly heading for a fail in my final year.

Norman saw this and, without any fuss (or fees), he gave me one to one tutorials after school for weeks on end. I took it for granted. It was school.

Years passed and I often wondered where Norman had gotten to. Occasionally, I would search him online, but nothing came up. I tried again and saw some vague reference to a Norman Davey and a garden centre. That would not be him, he was a teacher. It continued to quietly agitate me.

I looked again.

This garden centre was in Milltown, near the city. I went in search but there was no garden centre. I assumed it had been and gone and given way to new apartments that were everywhere. I gave up.

About two years ago, I went back to Mount St. Josephs to breathe in the timeless memories. I decided to return home a different route. A mile away from the school, a sign said, 'Milltown Garden Centre'.

Surely not, drive on. No, turn back, find out.

I drove in. A beautiful place close to the Little Brosna River. I was unsure what to do, what to say, how to say it.

A tall, handsome young man saw my uncertainty and came forward to help. He was cut out of his Dad.

Eventually, I asked him if Norman was his Dad. I was almost afraid of the answer.

Paul did not miss a beat.

He said, "Do you mean that man over there?".

Working away, a young, healthy-looking Norman Davey. He really had not changed. I introduced myself and then he did remember.

For me, it was emotional because this man was a God to me and, though I am sure he was kind to everyone, he took extra care of me.

As our conversation ended, I said that I was sure he would not remember me because I was struggling with French and he would remember the bright sparks, not the strugglers.

"No, Conor, it is the students that struggled that I remember the most. They needed the teacher more."

It is a simple sentence that gave me a great insight. All these years later, Norman is still teaching me.

As I left, I promised him copies of some earlier books. In his understated humble way, he said that would be nice. We said goodbye for now and I walked to my car.

"And, by the way, Conor, when I get those books, I'll be checking the grammar."

9: Understanding Your Power and Authority

In our work, family, and social life, we display and exercise power and authority at some point. Critically, we are sometimes aware of it and sometimes we have no idea that we have exercised it. And if I may reinforce a recurring theme in this book, it is that we know what we say and do but often we do not know the impact. Sometimes, responding to authority is an artificial response that can easily mislead and, at its worst, create rapid conflict.

Understanding the impact of your power and, in certain situations, your authority, is important to navigate life, work and friends in an empathetic and kind way.

We are always three people:

- We are who we think we are;
- We are who others think we are;
- We are who we are.

Our senses are driven by two brains:

- The rational; and
- The emotional.

How we perceive and how we are perceived is a combination of both the people we are and our brains.

Thankfully, today's world is more aware of the impact we can have on mental health, well-being and happiness. This is especially true at work, where many of us closely guard our private life and offer only our professional self. That can lead to assumptions about who we are – in most cases, those assumptions are wrong.

There are two discernible kinds of people and one of them is disastrous in a position of power.

Ivor Kenny, Can You Manage?

Peter and Prisoners

We noticed an increasing interest in mental health amongst our clients, and especially amongst our younger workshop participants. It led to a need to develop an influential and actionable course in well-being and mental health. After a long search, we met Peter, who leads and delivers this.

Peter is an interesting man. He has been at the forefront of dealing with and counselling those suffering addiction, and knows the challenges that mental health can bring. His background has brought him to the sharpest edges of society's most vulnerable and a story Peter told me triggered a thought that led to this chapter.

One of the most hopeless places anyone can ever be is in the strict confines of a prison cell. Besides the obvious fears, it must feel like the bottom rung of whatever ladder the prisoner was on.

A prison boss wanted to teach some of his wardens to engage better with long-term prisoners so that they might have a more positive horizon to think about and enjoy.

Peter replied, saying, "So, you want them to learn about motivational conversations and interventions?".

The boss agreed and Peter paused. A smart question was coming: "But before I do that, do your officers understand the influence and power of their authority on a prisoner before they even begin to talk to them?".

The boss wanted clarification: "What do you mean?".

Peter replied, "If I am a long-term prisoner, a prison officer to me is authority. They can lock me up, put me in segregation, deprive me of my privileges and even raid my cell wearing full riot gear with a bunch of fellow officers. My point is that there is a need to understand how the officer is being perceived before he even thinks about now being the person who motivates".

Before we can jump in to be that motivational force, we must consider the other person's belief of who we are, what we represent to them, our power and what our authority says to them. Inevitably, that is not obvious, but it is certain to influence their thinking and their response.

At work, how we communicate will be artificial because our primal instinct is to protect our job. Whilst that will always get an answer, we cannot always know if it is real or based on a different hidden agenda.

Maslow's Hierarchy of Needs

Abraham Maslow was an American psychologist best known for producing 'Maslow's hierarchy of needs', which was his theory of good mental health based on fulfilling our human needs in order of priority, allowing us to become who we are.

But behaviour in the human being is sometimes a defence, a way of concealing motives and thoughts, as language can be a way of hiding your thoughts and preventing communication.

Abraham Maslow

He named five fundamental needs. They start with the physiological needs and work up to self-actualisation:

- Physiological: These are fundamental needs such as food, water, air, air, shelter, clothes, warmth, reproduction, and sleep;
- Safety and security: When our most basic physiological needs are met, we move to the need for safety and security, which can be met by being in a society with structure, law and order, as well as a strong family unit;
- Love and belonging: This is the need to belong, the need for interpersonal relationships, friendships, and love;
- Esteem: This is our desire for achievement. Maslow named two types: achievement for oneself and the desire for external respect from others;
- Self-actualisation: This means reaching one's full potential.

If we understand this hierarchy, especially in those who we are trying to communicate with, it will go a long way to understanding their perspective and showing real empathy.

Culture

Culture is one of those throwaway words that people tend to use freely. Often, they are confusing culture with values – the two are entirely different. I struggled to explain the difference but a friend and fellow board member of a shared charitable interest gently shared a line that sums it up perfectly. He said, "Culture is that which keeps the herd roughly moving from east to west". And if that culture is flawed, then so is the behaviour.

What is the Difference between Culture and Values?

Values are the foundation stones upon which a business or relationship is built. They do not shift; they are constant. It is no different in a family home.

Culture, on the other hand, does shift and moves in response to everything happening around us.

Values set the tone. They are simply the non-negotiable things that really matter to a family, a club, a company, or any unit of people who need to be aligned and behind similar beliefs and goals.

What Is Emotional Intelligence?

Emotional intelligence is simply your ability to understand and control your own emotions, inner conflicts, and later behaviour, along with understanding the emotions of other people.

Emotional intelligence has three fundamental imperatives:

- First, the ability to be emotionally aware and really understand your own emotions and be able to label them objectively – for example, fear, stress, euphoria, grief, love and so on;

- The second aspect is the ability to use these emotions in the best way possible and manage them effectively – a simple example is controlling a simmering temper;
- Third, an ability to identify emotions in others and empathise appropriately.

Emotional intelligence is generally said to include at least three skills:

- Emotional awareness, or the ability to identify and name one's own emotions;
- The ability to harness those emotions and apply them to tasks like thinking and problem-solving; and
- The ability to manage emotions, which includes both regulating one's own emotions when necessary and helping others to do the same.

If we stop and look at the leaders who have made an impression on us, we always see that they can balance and manage their thoughts, actions and behaviour. These are primary leadership qualities and when we think of bad bosses, the contrary is the case.

10: LISTENING, SILENCE, AND WATCHING

Grace and Graciousness

This is the dictionary definition of 'graciousness': it is courteous, kind, and pleasant, especially towards someone of lower social status.

Grace has been my partner in business for 15 years and her parents could not have chosen a more appropriate name. Grace is gracious. Grace is patient, calm, understated, a remarkably high achiever and modest.

Sometimes, oversized egos love the idea of engaging with a gracious listener. They can rattle on for hours, enjoying the sound of their own voice, oblivious to the real impact they are making. Of course, what they think and what we think are two vastly different perspectives.

We were at a meeting many years back. Though incredibly charming at first, he sensed the graciousness. Loving the sound of his own voice, he reminded me of a bad driver in rush hour traffic. As soon as Grace began to speak, he hit the throttle, screeched the tyres, and pulled out in front of her, slowing down to enjoy the control. At least, that is how my brain saw it. Regardless, Grace was gracious, though I was getting angry.

The meeting finished and we left, graciously, of course. There was silence as we walked to our cars. I wanted to see whether Grace would unleash some pent-up frustration and be ungracious in her view. No, it did not happen, and it was never going to happen.

There was a reason.

I brought up in conversation the man who could not listen. Naively, I said to Grace, "How come you let that man cut across you every time you went to speak?"

Grace did not bat an eye: "His desire to speak and be heard was far greater than mine, Conor, and it's all in the proposal anyway".

In the end, as Grace predicted, he read our document and joyfully announced he would say "Yes".

Sadly, we said "No".

Sometimes, early warning signals can save you a lot of distress down the road.

Listening

When we speak, we are repeating what we already know.

When we listen, we learn something new.

There is a difference between listening and hearing.

Really listening means to pay close attention to what is being said underneath the words. We listen, not just to what someone says, but to figure out who they are. In some ways, the important thing is to listen to what has not been said.

Sometimes, we think we have listened, but we have not; we have been present in a parallel universe.

People can look like they are listening, but they are churning over what it is they want to say. Observe the body language in any group of people and you will quickly spot what I mean.

Of course, the danger with not listening is that some people will listen to a version of your story but understand something completely different. This is the illusion that communication had taken place.

Listening is one of the greatest gifts anyone can give. For some, it is natural; for others (including me), it is a skill that needs work, discipline and reprogramming our default ear.

They have the unique ability to listen to one story and
understand another.

Pandora Poikilos

They Had No Idea

I love to run. It is a pastime that has rewarded me in so many ways, so often. Running people have common threads and universally, they are not driven by ego, but by humility and the ability to enjoy something difficult, challenging and exhausting.

Like every village, runners have the mix that every society shares.

I loathe the start of a long run. For me, for the first few miles, I need space and peace until my reluctant natural rhythm kicks in and accepts we need to work together for the next hour or two.

I like to listen, and I enjoy the battles for attention – the joker, the grumpy, the optimist, the trouble spotter and all the characters that are bonded, in this case, by the love of long-distance running.

Running equalises. You might have the biggest house or bank balance, but nobody cares. You are there for who you are, how you run and nothing else. It is an ego-free sport and that is why it grounds us so richly.

Like sheep following an un-appointed leader, someone sets off and we follow. It is a lottery. In a large group, you will end up running with someone who is your pace, your speed and who is or isn't having a good day. As the run lengthens, that shifts and sometimes, you will be alone; that is often welcome too.

We were off and I was in the middle finding my own natural rhythm. A little bunch in front were just a tiny bit too fast for now. A little group behind, just that bit too slow. I had a two-metre bubble around me, and it suited me fine.

Behind were two good friends. Lovely people but not gifted with the best listening skills ever.

On a long run, often described as the ultimate mindfulness, it can be fun to tune in to the moment and let your imagination rest away from troubled thoughts. I decided to listen in to the two behind.

They were chatting freely, both, at the same time, parallel. I was smiling. Here was a perfect example of talking and not listening. I glanced at my watch and we were 15 minutes in. They were both effortlessly talking in utterly parallel moments.

Around the next corner and a hill. No matter how fit or fast you are, this hill kills you. It is short, it is steep, and it bites. I knew they would not be able to talk their way up.

Silence. The talking stopped as gravity had its way.

Over the hill and some respite, breathing recalibrated, lactic acid slipping away, rhythm restored.

One turned to the other ready for the next chapter. We were 20 minutes in.

"What were you saying?", said A to B.

"I can't remember", said B in reply.

They laughed together and said it must not have been important, but they had gotten through the opening miles and they were having fun.

The Introvert and the Extrovert

Part of the skill in delivering a good workshop is the ability to listen. For some people, that is interpreted to mean biting their lip and forcing themselves to stay silent. That is not listening; that is hearing.

But it is easy to label someone as a good or bad listener without helping them understand the impact. Involving people is how they understand. Just telling them does little.

I was reading something about listening and then I saw two short lines that improved my own listening ear threefold. It makes sense, it is clear, and it is a terrific way of understanding why we sometimes need to simply stop talking.

Extroverts need to talk to think. Introverts need to think to talk.

Unknown

Take a moment, process it slowly, and then practice it forever.

And Then It Went Dead

In London, in the mid-90s, I wanted to come home. After nine years, I had enough.

Work was scarce, very scarce. Worse still, this was pre-technology days – hard to imagine for today's youth. No Internet, no WhatsApp, no email, no FaceTime, no Zoom, and no mobiles. Car phones were just taking off, but they were very expensive to buy, install and use. It was mail, stamps, and the post office. If you had a landline, you were privileged but for me, it was the trusty red phone box, the Tardis of its day.

You saw a newspaper advert – remember, no Internet then – you wrote a letter, you sent it off, you waited and waited and waited. The answer was always "No", though most did not even bother to tell you. The excitement of a branded envelope, followed by the equal low.

It was hard to keep going and money was running out.

At last, a glimmer of hope.

It was a well-established business, neither where I wanted it to be nor in an industry I would have chosen but it was a job.

The short message said, "Call me at 3:15pm on Thursday next to discuss".

My first concern was securing the phone box. I did, with an Oscar-winning performance of a busy man talking to no one.

At 3:15 pm, I call. I get through. He is clearly on speaker and I am imagining a small, powerful man with his shoes on the desk, cigar in hand, rocking back and forth. In a heavy accent, he said, "Tell me your story".

I began slowly, logically and trying my best to give him good reasons to take things forward. I was intuitively happy that I was doing the best I was able to do. There was silence at the other end, interrupted only by the occasional whisper or unidentifiable noise.

I was mid-way through my background with not much more to say when he interrupted, "I won't detain you any longer".

With that, he was gone.

Patience and focus were not in abundance for the little man with the big desk.

It is always worth letting someone get to the end of their story.

That is always where the truth is revealed and where we might not have predicted what we thought early on.

Checking Out

It was one of the big brand hotels in the UK. Functional, soulless, and anonymous. It was busy and full of businesspeople in a perpetual rush. I went to bed in room 205.

At 2:30 am, a loud banging on my door. He was very drunk and convinced the love of his life was inside. Even my clearly masculine voice did not convince him otherwise.

I decided to call reception, but the phone was broken. At 2:55 am, he gave up. I drifted to sleep. At 3:15 am, he was back. Oh God.

Using my mobile, I rang the hotel. The night porter answered, "I'm sorry, sir, but I can't leave my desk".

It was 4:00 am before I found peace.

It had been a horrible night and all I wanted to do was escape the hotel. I queued for 15 minutes along with all the other grey-suited men. Finally, I got to the desk. The girl never lifted her head: "Your room number, please?", followed by a slow "Ah yes, Mr. Kenny".

Still, her head was face down. Then came: "And how was your stay with us?".

I deliberately paused to emphasise my reply. I replied with one word: "Brutal".

"Wonderful, Mr. Kenny. So we will look forward to seeing you again soon."

The Invisible Man

I am often intrigued by the plain lack of awareness of some professionals when a customer is in their field of vision or even standing right in front of them, patiently waiting to be noticed.

One such true scenario struck me powerfully and I found myself writing a little story so I could capture those invisible moments. This is it:

Have you seen me?
I am that regular customer who is often in your place. I am a little shy, normal, and very patient.
I am so patient that I watch with a slight soft smile as your staff dash here, dash there, but never notice me.
Sometimes I look on and watch your staff enjoying a little gossip. I smile then too. They do not realise that I can hear them, and I am amazed they do not even see me. It's funny though, because sometimes they are gossiping about their company, their boss, their job and even about those

'nasty little creatures' we call customers. Yet, they never see me standing right under their nose and listening to their every word.

As the invisible man I see everything, but those beautifully dressed professionals seem to see nothing. Often, I will go into a beautiful comfortable reception area. I will admire the expensive furniture, the features, and the beautiful paintings, but I will wonder too. I will wonder if the smart receptionist with the smart uniform is alive ... or maybe just another feature? I will marvel at the speed they chew gum. I will wonder why they are obsessed by their nails, pc, or phone, and I will be amazed at how they never even notice my entrance or my presence!

To many, I am just that ordinary guy we call the guest, the client, or the customer. But, to my friends, family, and colleagues, I am a little more than that, I might even be a little bit special. You see, I am that regular average guy who everyday makes the wheels of industry turn. There are lots of me, in fact thousands and millions. I represent the majority, not the few, and I represent the invisible customer everywhere.

But I am smiling my wry smile again. Any idea why? Thing is, I am not stupid, though invisible to you, I do see everything. I also see choice, options, and alternatives ... and ... I know my 'rights'. I have just exercised those 'rights' and guess what? ... I will not be back, no matter what.

Why am I still smiling my wry smile? Well, it tickles me that every day and every year your company spends so much money advertising for me to come to you. Funny thing is, if you had opened your eyes in the first place, I was already there! ... But now, I am gone.

My Mum Stole a Car

Perhaps not in the true sense of the term, but let me explain.

My Mum grew up on a small farm in a very remote part of the west of Ireland. Her Dad was a police officer and the farm a parallel life.

Nearby lived a favourite cousin, where many hours were spent playing and working. Adding to the excitement, the cousin's father had a car. Remember, this was just after World War Two. The car, a much-prized possession then, was housed in a barn and, in a sign of more innocent and safe times, the key was left on a nail in the shed.

My Mum wanted to drive and along with her co-accused, she 'borrowed' it occasionally, being incredibly careful to park it back in the barn exactly from where they left. Over time, they were proud of their stealth and the father never seemed to notice – certainly he never said a word.

And then.

One day, they were playing in the barn that doubled up as a garage. The father walked in very slowly. Strange, this was out of character. He looked at them both with a sharp focused stare, left to right, right to left. Not a word. Quietly, he looked at the key and returned to look at the two girls. The key was unhooked and slipped into his pocket. A last glance and he was gone. Not a word. Not one word.

My Mum still tells me this story and it is a great way to illustrate that sometimes silence is more powerful than an outburst of words and, in her case, the impact has lasted a long lifetime.

Of course, what myself and my brother have yet to share is that we too followed her example – aged 12.

11: THE UNFORTUNATE LAST WORD

Creating Pain

When we are young, we do not yet understand the consequences of some of our actions. It is a part of growing up and it is only through experience that we learn what not to do. In some ways, days that are not burdened by overthinking the consequences of our words or actions are carefree days, meaning we did not care, think about caring or think through what we did. We just forgot about it. That does give youth a defence of sorts but certainly not an adult.

Like you, I have witnessed events that were shocking and read emails that are forever in print and etched on my mind.

Whilst they might sting momentarily, the long-lasting memory is of the person, never the content. That memory is unlikely to ever change. Worse still, it can quickly become a story that spreads easily.

Going back to being emotionally intelligent, it is that short-term egoic satisfying moment that allowed the author to press Send. Whilst the satisfaction might be electric, it is doomed to be short-lived. The memory of it is quite the opposite.

No matter how deep the insult, no matter how true or false, people get over these easily and quickly. The person who fired the bullet suffers far longer. Why? Because of an amazingly simple and obvious piece of logic. When we create a problem, we create pain.

Imagine you have a right of way in traffic. A car with an over-excited teenager cuts you up. He is in the wrong, legally and morally. You feel an intense need to remind him. At the next traffic lights, you get out of your car and approach his. He opens the window. You make your point. He hurls extreme abuse. You threaten him. He gets out of the car. Onlookers stop and stare. The police are called. Traffic at a standstill, tempers rising and then what? Then, you have created pain. This is a maxim that applies to any interaction driven by ego or uncontrolled emotions. We have all seen them and we remember them.

If we are wise, we will remember this simple truth before we allow our emotions to escape and go wild.

Maybe all one can do is hope to end up with the right regrets.
Arthur Miller, The Ride Down Mt. Morgan

The Late Night Email

Sometimes, in business, we make the unfortunate mistake of taking on work that we should not have. We all do it and we all get caught by the wrong people from time to time.

Wrong is a strong word and, of course, subjective, but wrong for you and me simply means that our values are not aligned. That inevitably leads to a parting. It is not wrong to ignore your intuition or, at the very least, acknowledge the alarm bells ringing in your head.

I ignored mine, even though the warning signs were there.

He wanted to meet in advance of a specific assignment. This was normal. The briefing was not. In the briefing, his focus was on the personalities of his team, rather than on their performance or competency. He had a gift for trouble-spotting their flaws and no words of admiration, praise, or empathy. He bordered on paranoia and every point was about bolstering his position.

He saw ghosts and threats that did not exist.

The next morning, we went to work. It was a focused and successful day, reaching the goal we had all set out to achieve.

Months later, we were asked to come back and do more.

This time, we paused. Intuition said this was not a good idea.

Late one afternoon, we wrote a note to say that with regret, we would be unable to accept the assignment. We thanked them for the work we had done and wished them well. We had no doubt it was the right thing to do both morally and commercially. In business, most deals fail. That is the ebb and flow of commercial life.

One evening, I received an email. It was full of mistakes, sentences that did not make sense and you could almost see the wine stains. It was horrific and one a lawyer would have enjoyed feasting on.

My own desire to respond was not about to create goodwill and I found myself writing a reply to his rambling note, line by line.

I have always lived by the notion that you review anything you are about to send. You take all the emotion out, stick with the facts and edit wherever necessary. It is a discipline worth having.

I read my reply slowly and, after making sure that I was being factual and unemotive, I decided to scrap it.

Instead, I wished him every good fortune and thanked him for the note.

Whilst his email will live long in our memory, our response is one we can always stand over. And the moral? Do not spill your wine over your keyboard and do not press Send when you wipe it down.

Wine stains on keyboards are extremely hard to remove.

The Grenade Thrower

The role of the human resources manager is challenging. They are the bridge between what the boss wants and the employee. They are the peacemaker and they bear a lot of responsibility. They are often a shoulder to lean on and they need exceptional patience.

Many years ago, I worked for a large company. The human resources manager was as nice a person as you could meet. Patient, cheerful, obliging and on top of her brief. Her office was more like a domestic living room and reflected her warm homely nature. It was an oasis in a busy environment.

Unexpectedly, word went around that, after 14 years, Maria was to leave. It seemed she was leaving into an uncertain future and this added to the mystery, as she was not in the first flush of youth.

Like most corporates, there was a standard procedure when someone was leaving the company. A little after-work drink, some flowers to go with the pleasant words, a few memories and the inevitable cut glass fruit bowl. To a young gun, it was not the most exciting event to attend but duty called.

We were to assemble at 5.30 pm. And off we would go. At 5.00 pm in my tiny office, I heard an out of place commotion. I had no idea what was happening, but someone was roaring and shouting, and tempers were running free. It was time to keep my head down and press on.

The tiny door to my tiny office burst open. Outside stood Maria, red-faced and raging. She stared at me and I can only describe it as that moment when a bank robber looks at you to decide whether you are to be a hostage or not. I was stunned. The stare seemed to last forever. I had nothing to say. Something was wrong.

"You are all right. Goodbye, Conor" and my door closed.

I let my heart rate settle and felt my mouth dry. Maria weaved her way in and out of every desk dispensing her view of each employee. Most were out of favour and were told plainly what she really thought of them.

It was shocking and it was funny. You could hear yourself listening to her loud assessments and going "I agree" to some and "That is true but a little harsh" to others.

We could all argue that she was being truthful and that may be the case. Sadly, it is not the memory for anyone caught in her fire. After 14 years, this was her legacy and the only thing anyone ever remembered about her.

It took 14 years to build a superb reputation and less than 10 minutes to destroy it.

History Repeating

We rarely remember the words, but we remember their impact as well as their actions.

I was doing a little interviewing on behalf of a big public company in the financial services sector. My regular commissioning contact was a small middle-aged man who, it seemed to me, led a lonely life. He was a good guy and worked hard, dedicated to his job and loyal to his employer. He blended in modestly.

It was the final interview for a senior position and the candidate had already been through two interviews which she passed with flying colours. We met in the lobby. The group chief executive, my contact, and the candidate.

She was elegant, perfectly dressed and had an aura that said confidence was not in short supply.

We walked that awkward walk to the chief executive's splendid office, and I listened to the artificial chit-chat along the way.

I could feel the wind from her fluttering eyelashes.

We went in.

I decided to watch, listen, and learn before saying anything.

She conducted herself with supreme confidence and knowledge. It was going very well.

But I was not convinced. It seemed too smooth, far too smooth.

Time came to ask a few questions and I was keen to ask something that would reveal a little more than the stock answers of an experienced finance professional. She had forgotten something.

I asked her if she could take me through her career to date and her personal highlights. She glided through a well-rehearsed path and it was convincing and compelling – but there was a flaw. I knew who she was. We were both employees of the same company in London at separate times.

As I watched her polished interview ending, I asked her if there was anything else she wanted to add. She said "No" and that she was happy with all she had heard.

I asked her again if there was anything missing from her resume. "Absolutely not" came the fast reply.

I did not answer. I sat in silence and, for the first time, she seemed uneasy. It was time to act.

"I am a little confused. You appear to have worked at this company for three years but were they not the same three years you worked for company X, which does not appear on your resume?"

She stared hard. Her eyes fixed. She knew I knew something. She did not know what. She turned the hose on me. She said I must be confusing her with someone else. I said I did not think so. She stared again and with considerable elegance, stood up and said:

"Clearly, I am being confused with someone else by this man who I have never met in my life before. I do not know who he is or why he is questioning my integrity and, if this is a trick at interview to see how I would respond, then my career speaks for itself. My career in finance and banking is beyond approach and I have no need to convince you otherwise. If this is the suspicious and dreadful way you treat high achieving, honest finance executive candidates for senior positions, then I am sure you will understand that your culture and attitude are beneath what I am looking for. We are not a match. I will not be joining you. Goodbye."

It is easy to be hypnotised by the performance, the words or even the elegance. However, the art of interviewing successfully also must rise above the intuitive, the sensory and the visible.

Good interviews elicit interesting reactions and that is why any communication that is ever exploring a key decision always must combine the science with the art.

Relying only on intuition is a gamble. Relying only on fact misses out on understanding the person, their drive and, most of all, whether they are a good fit for you, your colleagues and your business.

The Man with Seashells

Early in my career, I was interviewed by a kindly consultant who was retained by my future boss to weed out the good from the bad. That was a wise move. He was an astute, calm, deep sort of chap. I admired him, and I admired his judgement, skill, and intuition. He told me this story that I have always employed in one of those 'intuitive' situations.

Your intuition is a particularly useful tool, but it can have the occasional blip. Be careful.

It was the final interview for a senior sales director's role. The earlier candidates I interviewed were uninspiring. I would not have offered any of them the job. Then, as the day was ending, in came 'Mr. Perfect', sharp, bright, immaculate, calm, warm and so on. In my mind, he already had the job.

After the interview, he got up to leave. I was drawn to the beautiful leather briefcase and also to the very strange sound it made. As Mr. Perfect was about to leave, I asked him what that strange sound was. He beamed from ear to ear and said:

"I'm so glad you asked me that question. It's my collection of seashells. I bring them everywhere with me".

68

He did not get the job.

Intuition is great but even better is to combine the art with the science.

12: Preparing

One important key to success is self-confidence. An important key to self-confidence is preparation.

Arthur Ashe

In youth, certainly my youth, I spent enormous hours figuring out how to take short cuts at work. Looking back, I had the innocence to believe that all those old people were misguided and that a cropped version of something was just as good as the full length.

I was wrong.

In business, especially in sales, there can be a culture of 'winging it' and lazy people have done their best to turn this into a virtue. I know, I tried. But I was lucky enough to realise that winging it often meant coming back to earth with a nasty bump.

We all have simple lightbulb moments that help us unwittingly to change track. They are moments of awakening. Mine was incredibly simple.

Alan

Early in my career in London, I worked for an exceptionally fine German company. I was a salesperson along with another 11. We were all young, well paid, working for an excellent brand in beautiful offices and, at that stage of life, we had nice company cars. They certainly knew how to attract eager and energetic young men. Most of all, it was fun. Not so much because the senior team wanted that to be the culture, but 12 young men did.

As often as we could, we reassured one another that there was no need to do this or that; the goal was to get through as much of the day as was necessary and then head out in pursuit of fun.

Each of us were highly measurable and figures did not lie. I was somewhere in the middle, doing just enough to keep funding my life of fun. Whatever money was coming in was going out just as fast. In youth, you are never going to grow old, run out of money or get swept away in some sudden storm you never saw coming.

There is comfort in a pack and inevitably someone would suggest another lunchtime or late afternoon walk on the wild side. We all followed, but one man did not.

Alan was as nice a guy as you could meet. Cheerful, energetic, and bright. Every time we headed off for another boozy lunch, Alan would decline. Instead, he would wave a cheerful goodbye and encourage us to have fun. I especially remember Alan at his desk with his head down, working hard. He was constantly on the telephone chatting with his many customers.

On the surface, we thought: "How boring".

Deep down, we admired him. He did not need to follow the pack. He worked hard, extremely hard, alien to the rest of us. He prepared, he was perpetual motion and a man with little time for idle chit-chat. He came in early, he left late, and he was always focused.

Looking back, combining his energy, his work ethic, his cheerful positive nature, his single mindedness, it will come as no surprise to hear that Alan was the top salesperson every single year that I worked with him.

Winging it might be fun but, if I were you, if you want success, adopt Alan's values – and do it early.

Getting Away With It. Just.

Getting a big deal is a big deal in a business.

Together with my colleagues, we were close to the biggest deal ever. If we succeeded, we would have a blue-chip major company to add to an impressive client list, but it was not going to be easy. There was a lot to do and preparation needed to be meticulous.

My boss was a stickler for detail and would not go into any presentation without perfect preparation. It is a lesson that has served me well ever since.

We were to meet the board of a well-known UK company in a city centre hotel at 7.00 pm and on to dinner at 7.30 pm.

My boss, a perfectionist, and understanding the strategic importance of this, made sure we were ready. An external consultant was commissioned to prepare a plan and I was to present it.

I had gotten to know this consultant well over the years. He was as bright as they come and a gentleman. Anything he produced would be compelling. It was a good move by my boss.

But our favourite consultant had one chink in his armour, time keeping was not his forte.

We were to meet at 4:00 pm to run through the presentation, rehearse it and, most importantly, understand it.

4:00 pm came and went. So too 5.00 pm and then 6.00 pm. No sign of our man. Nerves were getting fraught. With 15 minutes to go to our meeting, still no sign. At 7:00 pm, on the dot, our very British brand and very British executive arrived. Still no sign.

We exchanged conversation and we did our best to stall events. At 7.05 pm, a door opened and in came our man, windswept and apologetic. He handed me the thick beautifully-bound document and fled.

I was asked to sit at the head of the table. Time did not allow me read anything other than the front cover. Silence came and our British guests were all ears.

I invited them to open page 1, and I guided them through to the end at page 20.

Then came the worst moment.

After a pause, I asked them whether they had any questions.

Their pause lasted forever and then their chairperson said, "No, I think you have anticipated and answered all of our questions. We are happy to confirm your appointment. Let us go celebrate".

Of course, what they never knew was that I too was reading it for the first time parallel to them. Worse still, I read passages that I had absolutely no idea what they meant.

We had a great night and my boss, a man of few words, was in high spirits.

We said our goodbyes and a wave of exhaustion came over me. I walked the quiet city centre streets with my boss. He never said a word. I came to my car before his. As I was about to get in, I felt a light clap on my back ,"Well done". With that, he was off into the night and I swore I would never wing it again.

More Winging It

In the early years of this new century, I had the most wonderful job working with The Irish Pub Company. Founded by my boss, Mel McNally, in collaboration with Guinness, he created the global phenomenon of the Irish Pubs abroad concept. It was an extremely exciting and incredibly happy six years, fulfilling everything I wanted in my next career move. More on this later.

The concept attracted daily media interest and working there was a perpetual roller coaster. As part of my brief, I was also to manage group public relations. Great if you know what you are doing but daunting if you do not understand it. It was a steep and exciting learning curve, another measure of my boss who had great faith in his employees and gave them incredible freedom. He knew how to teach, and I learnt more in my six years working with him than from all my earlier jobs put together.

The daily tasks inevitably included press queries about the latest opening, whether it was in Las Vegas, China, or even inside the Arctic Circle. Over time, you learn the craft and begin to understand the difference between a story, publicity, and noise. With experience and applied learning, you get confident. Sometimes, that confidence can be too loose.

Many of us remember the famous Guinness images of the toucan, the zookeeper, and the pints of stout. They were created by John Gilroy, known as the portrait artist of the Queen of England and other heads of state. The work he is most famed for, however, is the iconic Guinness artwork of the 1930s, 1940s and 1950s.

Inevitably, when we opened a new pub in an exotic location, the toucan and Gilroy images were an essential ingredient in reproducing the atmosphere of an authentic Irish pub.

It did not take long before astute dealers and traders saw the rising value. Unintentionally, I was about to add to that.

An article appeared in a national newspaper extolling the investment value of authentic Gilroy pieces. Quickly, a prime-time morning radio programme noticed it. A call came, "Could you send someone in to be interviewed about Mr. Gilroy's rising tide?" We said "Yes" and I was dispatched at short notice.

Pat Kenny, no relation, is my favourite broadcaster. He is always on top of his subject and, unlike yours truly that day, he is prepared. He has those rare qualities of saying less and getting his guests to talk more, an art form that continues to decline in younger, less skilful broadcasters. His questions are sharp and his mind even sharper.

I arrived at the studios to be met by a researcher. We had the usual chat and then she asked me a very straight question: "How much do you know about Gilroy?". I could feel myself blush. "Not a lot." Here I was about to go into the most famous Irish broadcaster's studio. The man I admired so much. The man on top of his subject and I was about to go in as 'an expert' who knew nothing.

She looked at me with a raised eyebrow: "I thought so. Here, read this".

On a sheet in front of me were a thorough list of facts on Gilroy. I was still reading them as I entered the tiny studio. Of course, the wonderful thing about radio is no one can see you. If they did, they would have seen a head buried in a fact sheet with little eye contact with my hero host.

The interview went well, and a tape recording gave no hint of my ignorance. I had been saved from a catastrophic embarrassment. Once the interview was over and the ad break came, my gracious host finally got my full attention. He laughed and said, "Well done, Conor, and thank God for fact sheets and astute researchers".

There is an epilogue to this story about winging it and a warning too.

When I got back to the office, it would have been normal to have had three or four telephone calls waiting to be returned. This time, there were over 70. I had no idea what this was all about.

The calls varied in style.

"Please call Mrs. Smyth in Cork on …"

"Can you ring Billy urgently on …?"

"Please tell Conor that Mary Collins in Bundoran would like to speak with him as soon as possible."

I read every single message, and, for a very moment, I thought I had found stardom. The first and second calls I returned put paid to that notion fast.

I got through to Mrs. Smyth instantly. She was almost breathless. No chat. "I have a Gilroy ashtray. How much is it worth?" For reasons I still do not understand, I blurted out a low figure. Mrs. Smyth was disgusted. "Is that all?" Before I could say another word, the phone went dead.

Stupidly, I had yet to spot the pattern. I rang the next number. This time a man. It was Billy who wanted an urgent call. "I have a Gilroy lighter, an original. I even have the box for it. How much?" The current was flowing fast, and I was still stuck in this false expert world. I said something like, "If it is in good condition, you could expect to get €70".

There was an uncomfortable pause that felt more like a standoff and then: "You are some expert. You do not have a clue. Do not expect me to ever buy anything from your shop in future".

It was time to stop making calls and I was incredibly grateful there was no shop to buy from. If there was, I suspect a protest march would have set fire to it.

And the moral? Do not wing it and do not believe every radio guest is an expert, even if they appear as one.

13: Talking Nonsense

We read to learn. We read to be informed, and we read for pleasure. Listening is the same. If we make these a chore, then the reader and listener will disconnect and, unless it is essential, it is unlikely they will be in a rush to resume.

Whatever it is we want to say, it will be an immense help to the listener or reader if they can enjoy, understand, and benefit from your words.

Take this beautiful quotation. It illustrates this point perfectly. We should avoid writing and talking nonsense.

The books transported her into new worlds and introduced her to amazing people who lived exciting lives. She went on olden-day sailing ships with Joseph Conrad. She went to Africa with Ernest Hemingway and to India with Rudyard Kipling. She travelled all over the world, while sitting in her little room in an English village.

Roald Dahl, Matilda

Whether we talk or write, we are doing the same thing; they are simply different forms of communication, but the difference lies in including or excluding tone. What we say, and how we say it, says a lot about who we are.

An email full of errors catapults us to a conclusion that quickly cascades into a judgement that may not be at all correct.

A voice that we do not like, for some unknown reason, has the same impact. We judge, rightly or wrongly. Of course, only the content matters. It is the human condition that can prevent us seeing beyond the cover.

In life and in business, we use language in diverse ways. We can be formal, elegant, and so on, but it is informal language that can easily mislead. These are jargon, clichés, slang and swearing. They are each different.

What is Jargon?

The dictionary tells us jargon is: "special words or expressions used by a profession, industry, or group that are difficult for others to understand".

When you talk jargon, your customer may well be staring at you, but their mind has already taken flight and drifted far away from your best efforts to make them understand. This is especially true in business.

Jargon is dangerous for two reasons:

- First and critically, I will not understand what you said;

- Second, it damages your brand or how you are perceived.

Let me give you two online examples.

Something for the Weekend

2 x B&B subject to T&C and rate availability + 1 x Table D'hote Dinner x 2. (A La Carte Not Included). Rate is PPS with limited upgrade options but not inclusive of Spa or Aqua Centre access but inclusive of Leisure Centre off-peak access for Over 18s only.

Something to Sleep On

What's important in choosing your next time. The density of any polyfoam layers in lbs per cu. ft (lb/ft³). The percentage of natural rubber and synthetic rubber of any latex layers. The gauge of the coils, the number of the coils, and the density of any polyfoam edge support. If the quilting material is polyfoam or memory foam and is in the range of 'around an inch or so' or less, then it is not essential to know the density. If any quilting layers are 2" or more, then you need to know the density of any foam materials in the quilting.

There are only three outcomes after you have read these:

- The first is 'I understood';
- The second is 'I think I understood';
- The third is 'I did not understand'.

If your answer was the second or third choice, communication has not taken place and both parties have lost out.

If the first example had said: "A really good hotel weekend for two, including ...", then we would know more.

In the second example, what I really wanted to hear is that it is an exceptionally well-made mattress.

Simple is always good.

Slang

Jargon is not slang. Slang is simply informal language, while jargon is specific to a group of people or industry. Slang can be specific to a region or a country and usually there is a very thin thread connecting the word to the meaning. For example, 'a ton' in describing money is £100. Or 'they lost the plot' – if it were meant literally, we might offer to help them find it.

Many words we all use commonly fall into this category of language, which is great if you understand the true meaning behind the word. For example, we are all frequent users of terms such as 'telly', or 'dodgy' or 'cuppa' or 'it cost me an arm and a leg'. The list goes on. Most of these have fallen into our daily conversation but the more parochial we get, the more confusing to anyone outside that circle.

Take Cockney rhyming slang, which is a dialect particular to London. Its basis is that the spoken word rhymes with the real word. For example, 'apples and pears' mean stairs or 'dog and bone' means phone.

Whilst slang can be amusing, all too easily it can prevent communication being effective.

Swearing

Swearing is often unwittingly used to emphasise a point and sometimes is effectively a comma or full stop. Words that were once completely off limits have become more acceptable, but the question is always acceptable to whom?

We were asked to meet a minor celebrity who had a strong public presence along with a major ego. He, and his team, had spotted an opportunity to work with us on a project. We agreed to meet.

They had substance and skill and the project had possibilities. We were cautious. In business, more deals do not happen than do. We questioned and probed, asked and answered and then we were done.

As always, our small team gathered to discuss the meeting and what we wanted to do. In our group were two women and their presence taught a simple lesson that the men did not grasp.

Throughout the conversation, in the lobby of a stylish hotel, he swore, he cursed, and every second word he used would curl your toes. Whilst I heard the words, I was focused on the substance.

Women, with far better sensory powers than most men, heard them too. The difference was they also saw the reaction of those sitting around us and how their uncomfortable shuffling told us exactly what they thought.

After all, what is the point in working with a celebrity if he alienates half his market through words alone?

Clichés

It is a cliché that most clichés are true, but then like most clichés, that cliché is untrue.

Stephen Fry

Clichés have crept into the English language with increasing rapidity. A cliché is a phrase that is overused and betrays a lack of original thought or any real meaning. In some ways, they are the most interesting words to analyse. If you have been on a bus or train in near proximity to a group of young people, you can sit back and enjoy the experience of learning a whole new language that earlier generations would not understand.

Recently, someone asked me if I would write a small example to illustrate what I meant, especially in an office setting. This is what I wrote. Naturally, it is exaggerated.

Imagine bright young executives firing each other up in the boardroom before a sales meeting. Bradley launches into an excited monologue that might just go something like this:

"Hey, Ariana. Hey, Ivy. Hi, Guys. I'm looking forward to this little sales meeting pow wow? I have been burning the midnight oil to make sure all my ducks are in a row, but every cloud has a silver lining. You know me, when life gives you lemons, I make lemonade. We really need more outside the box thinking today, you know what I mean? Hop on the helicopter, admire the blue sky thinking then, once we see the LZ, land the helicopter, push the envelope, move forward, get some heavy lifting done early and then, in the final analysis, we can harvest the low hanging fruit, then go out there with the client and boil the ocean, keep the troops in the loop, so by the end of the day we can move forward faster and drink our own champagne. I am buzzing."

Clichés can talk, make noise, sound like something but they just confuse.

14: STRAIGHT TALKING

Sometimes we talk too much. Sometimes we confuse the simple. Sometimes we get lost. Straight-talking people do not like to waste time and do not worry too much about how their message is perceived. They just want to be clear, effective, and understood. Sometimes we do not like it but that is a reflection on our own innate sensitivity or insecurity, an emotional reaction.

When we do not like what they say, our natural response is to criticise them for being cold, blunt, or devoid of empathy. That is not true; that is our way of seeing it; for them, it is borne out of being honest and describing it so. Often, the straight answer is pure and free of emotional attachment. If we do not like it, that reflects more on us rather than them.

A stupid man's report of what a clever man says can never be accurate, because he unconsciously translates what he hears into something he can understand.

Bertrand Russell

Lawyers

If you do not like something, it is easy to be afraid of it.

Lawyers are experts in weaving frightening webs.

If you think about the cheerful brochure colours of your holiday company, the soft tones of a design company and the confident brass signage of a beautiful luxury hotel, their language and subliminal messages are designed to connect with your emotions and needs.

Now look at legal papers. They are neutral. They often use italics. They may have images of a crest and even the address says something to you. The message is that this is important, pay attention.

They might say something like this.

Dear Sir,
Pursuant to the agreement dated August 30th 20XX, I set forward
details of unresolved issues, contrary to clause 2b (1) Part 2.
Should you continue to delay a prompt resolution as set out in the
original schedule, we expressly reserve the right to pursue all available
and equitable legal remedies, including but not limited to instituting
formal litigation proceedings against you.
Yours faithfully,
Sue, Grabbit and Run, Solicitors

And if we translate it:

Dear Sir,
If you do not keep up with your payments, we will sue you.
Yours faithfully,
Direct & Blunt, Solicitors

Fred

Fred is one of my favourite people. Fred is a chef at the highest level. He works incredibly hard and is completely focused on his fine art.

Fred does not like to waste time. Work drives him.

We were working together for a well-known brand. They are extraordinarily successful, and, like all successful businesses, they were in constant pursuit of making things even better.

In steps Fred.

Fred arrived early to the restaurant. The owner was excited to meet Fred, his reputation went before him. The usual prelude of chit chat followed, and Fred stood to the side, arms folded, listening, and looking slightly bored with the casual conversation. As we spoke, on went his chef's whites and he was off. This was his domain and we were here to do a job. Effortlessly, he worked alongside the existing crew, who were on their best behaviour.

They cooked, he watched. He cooked, they watched. Each interested in the other, the expert at work.

When all was done, the owner, excited, wanted to know what Fred thought of their current offering: "Well, Fred, what did you think of our food?".

I knew Fred well enough to be ready for what was often unexpected.

Looking straight into his eyes, Fred answered, "Shit".

The owner was a little taken aback and wanted Fred to elaborate.

I was not so sure that was a great idea. It was too late.

"What do you mean, Fred?", he asked hoping for a more benevolent response. But Fred does not do anything other than straight talk.

"It is shit. That is it", he replied.

Sometimes kitchens can get extremely hot and if you do not like the heat, then it might just not be the place for you.

Priests

In an earlier era, the religious community oversaw many essential national institutions, the church, hospitals, and education. They were excellent managers and commercially astute. They also embraced their own education and professional development.

Many years ago, my Dad was working with a group of priests to help them prepare for a visit of the Pontiff. Perfectionist that he is, it was important that everything was thought out, planned and ready. That especially included what the priests were trying to say when the Pope came. With an international network of superb educators, he wanted the priests to really consider their message. Enter Mario, regarded as one of the greatest sales trainers in the USA.

The priests were punctual and perfectly groomed in their suits, collars, shiny shoes, and equally shiny well-oiled hair. They waited for Mario.

Five minutes late, the door storms open and Mario, in a suit and cowboy boots, arrives.

"Good morning, gentlemen. Tell me, exactly what are you guys selling?"

Like all simple questions, the answer was not so easy. It is a lesson that applies to each of us, every day.

15: WHAT ARE YOU SAYING?

The title of this book is deliberate. It does not ask: "What are you trying to say?", which might infer that you are struggling to say something. Instead, it asks what it is that you have already said but probes whether you might just have failed to communicate even if you think you did.

In business especially, from a selling or marketing perspective, or even in a simple interview setting, it is easy to see why we might 'think' we have communicated. But the only benchmark that has any meaning is: "Do they understand?".

If they do, great.

If you think they do, check.

If they do not, goodbye.

Acting is a form of confession.

Tallulah Bankhead

Talk to Whom?

Effective communication does not rely on jargon, clichés, slang or even pseudo-poetic rhymes.

Effective communication must have structure and cover the fundamentals.

It starts with "Who do we want to talk to?". This cannot be 'everyone' because, no matter how compelling your subject or message, there will always be a segment who have no interest in what you have to say. They are rejecters. For example, the most wonderful television advert promoting the luxury and haute cuisine of the world's best steak and beef restaurant will be wasted on vegetarians. An apartment with a high view is not going to connect with anyone who fears heights.

Talk about What?

The second question is what do you want to talk about? Again, a simple question but one full of trapdoors and few fire escapes.

I remember giving a workshop on this topic some years ago. There was a young man who enjoyed the limelight, and, at every available opportunity, he asked a question or, more often, said, "I disagree".

This is normal daily fare for anyone leading a workshop, but it did not take long before the other attendees begin to rebel. Still, in his own way, he was working it out and that was rewarding.

At this event, there were 22 people and each of them owned their own business. Everyone came with a desire to refine their own message and everyone wanted a slice of the day. I came to this point: "What exactly do you want to talk about to your potential customer? Remember two things: it must benefit them, and they must be interested. Make sure they 'understand' what you are trying to say".

Enthusiasm got the better of him and his hand was raised in an instant. "Yes, Peter, what exactly is it you would like to say to your customer?"

Chest out, he said, "We want to welcome you into a world of backward-compatible, device-driven technology and help you transform, embrace and enjoy a more meaningful understanding of how the digital age will allow you to make more money".

He sat down, looking terribly proud.

I glanced around the other 21 participants and there was silence.

I was on the verge of asking everyone if they understood what Peter meant.

The body language told me it was best to move on, and swiftly.

A sidebar, a little later, would help him into: "A new piece of technology that will make you more money".

Being Clear

Some people enjoy a long introduction to get to the heart of the matter, almost a drum roll in the mind and a build up to a revelation.

It influences the listener and quickly evokes an emotional response that is always hidden, ranging from: "Get on with it" to "This is boring" to "I'm losing interest" or even "This is really wasting my time".

Whilst we can enjoy extended stories in a social setting, they do not always work well in commerce, especially when people are busy. You are burning up their time without their permission.

Sometimes, it is far better to be clear: "Allow me get straight to the point".

Warming up people might make you more comfortable, but the chances are it will make the other person impatient.

But what you really need to consider before you open this jargon-free dialogue is this: Are you inadvertently going to talk about yourself or are you going to talk to them in a way that helps them?

Off on the Wrong Foot

Psychologists tell us that our favourite word, in any language, is our own name. Using names is a double-edged sword and sometimes swords end up in the wrong hands.

When I lived in London, I was damned by my name. Conor Kenny is easy to understand. In London, it did not seem so. I was Kenny Conor, Con O'Kenny, Connors Kennedy, Kenny O'Conor, Ken O'Connor and on it went. More on this shortly.

We were in the UK attending and collaborating on an expensive short course programme in a distinguished seat of learning and excellence. But excellence is one of those vague words that sounds good but is not so easy to measure. We want to believe the message to reassure ourselves that we made an excellent choice. Unwittingly, we pass judgement on excellence by the interaction with the people. The people become the brand and the brand is in the hands of their people. And this is the minefield that can easily explode the promise a brand makes, even if the other 99% is wonderful.

All meaningful interactions involve people and they define our significant memories.

My colleague, Grace, had put six months' work into getting the finer detail perfect. We were ready. Fourteen of us set off for London, a busy week lay ahead but it was exciting and a programme that would reward our own education.

Tristan wore a fine three-piece suit and his tie (which changed every day) gave reference to prestigious memberships, even if we did not know what they were. His accent was polished, and he knew his routine very well. We would be in Tristan's company on day 1 and day 3. Enough time to get to know a small group and enjoy the diverse opinions and personalities.

He gave a little introductory speech and went to great lengths to thank Grace for all her challenging work in getting everything to this point. He thanked Grace on at least six or seven occasions.

The only problem was that he called Grace by a different name each time. Grace became Grainne – and then a series of other names.

Whilst it was mildly irritating to all the delegates who knew Grace so well, it was not a big deal.

Not yet.

We had a coffee break and, recognising my own ability to confuse names from time to time, I had a quiet word with Tristan to tell him that 'Grainne' was in fact 'Grace'. He apologised and that was that. Or so we thought.

On day 3, Grace was haunted once more by Grainne and any time any of our colleagues mention that course, guess what the first memory is?

Getting names right matters and so does getting off on the right foot.

16: WHAT IS YOUR MESSAGE?

There is a difference between what you are trying to say and what your message is. I might want to tell you that you are about to lose your job, but my message is not simply: "You are fired". I might need to tell you that your engine needs an expensive repair, but my message may be that you will have another six years' carefree motoring. I might want a job, but my message is not going to be that initially. You might want a date but somehow, an opening line with the potential partner of your dreams might be more successful if you avoid: "Hello, my name is Theodore and I would like a date".

This means we must understand our purpose and our impact. If you throw a dart at a dartboard and you are .001 of a millimetre right of the bullseye, it is not the bullseye. Effective communication needs to be clear; by being clear, it will be understood. Your message and what you want to say are cousins; they are not siblings.

To be effective, we need to understand the difference and separate how we articulate them. To connect, they need to grab and hold our attention.

I bear messages which will make both your ears tingle.

Bram Stoker, Dracula

Faulty Cars

I was helping a friend with this very subject. He is a mechanic and a particularly good one. But business was not good.

His garage is on a terribly busy road with easy access, but he could not understand why he had such poor passing trade. Neither could I.

At lunchtime, we walked across the road for coffee. Walking back, I saw his huge sign dangling above the daily rush hour queues. It said: "Specialists in automotive diesel and petrol engines using ZRX2 diagnostic technology and fault screening".

It was a mouthful and though I might have thought I understood, I did not really.

Later, we changed it. The new sign said: "We fix faulty cars".

Overnight, his business improved.

A Boutique Hotel

The Atlantic coastline of Ireland is rugged, wild, and beautiful. It draws tourists in their thousands year after year. They follow worn paths and enjoy everything this unique landscape has to offer.

Many people in Ireland depend on tourism for their livelihood and, in a land not blessed with the consistency of Mediterranean sunshine, the focus has always been on the warmth of the people and ever-increasing food and accommodation standards. Competition is fierce and standing out from the crowd can be a significant challenge.

The well-worn tourist path is embedded in the big coach tour operator's routine. They go in a circle and one way. There are favoured stop-offs and photo opportunities, the place for morning coffee, some craft shops and, of course, B&B houses, hostels, guest houses, town houses, houses to rent, small hotels, big hotels, and luxury hotels. They cover the entire tourist population needs and they all compete.

Standing out from the crowd can be difficult.

If ever you took in this famous loop, it would not take long before you were comfortably numb and immune to digesting any further roadside messages. In a short space, they blur into nothingness.

Right at the end of one of the major tourist routes was a small and exceptionally beautiful boutique hotel. Unfortunately, by the time the day tripper got there, they had already overdosed on signage and beauty. It was easy to miss, even though it gave a fitting statement of perfection at the close of a touring day.

We were working with this beautiful hotel and their innovation, quality, standards, and delivery were superlative. For their size, they punched way above their weight.

They were creative and the tiny details added many cheerful moments to match the natural warmth and excellent dining.

Building the brand was easy, given the natural enthusiasm of the owners. Their website, beautifully written to capture the character of the hotel, stood out in language and style. The photography was superb and the overall message completely seductive.

We were all happy that it made the statement it wanted to make, and this hotel was not one to follow the crowd. Instead, they set a standard that would be hard to follow. That was intentional.

They opened their doors and it did not take long before they were busy and an instant hit with anyone who booked in. The future looked bright.

Typical tourist signs often over-promise nights of regal luxury. Exaggeration is not well-regulated. It does not take long before the very standard and far from original descriptions fade fast into an overloaded tourist's mind.

"Star of the Sea. Bed & Breakfast with luxurious *en suite* bathrooms, television, free Wi-Fi and sea views."

They have not altered in generations and it is easy to see why young generations cannot connect with these dated messages.

Three weeks after the boutique hotel opened, I was back in the hotel. As I pulled into the car park, it looked great – and then … from the corner of my eye, I could see one of those free-standing blackboards promising a beautiful interior to match the eye-catching exterior. That was OK; the message was not. It was the typical message favoured by the B&B brigade.

I went inside, met the owner, and asked whether they had a small axe to hand. The owner was perplexed, naturally and asked why. I told them I wanted to cut up the blackboard and use it for firewood. They laughed but they got it. Quick as a flash, they said, "What would you write instead?"

I was certainly on the spot. I took out a pen and pad and wrote three words: "Really nice bedrooms".

Some months later, on another visit, we laughed about the sign but there was a learning. The owner told me that regularly, people would come into reception and say, "We saw your sign" or "We would like to see the really nice bedrooms".

Over 10 years on, the sign is still there, and it is still doing its job.

A Good Night's Sleep

There is a danger that advertising can look good and sound great but, if it does not inspire and motivate the reader to act, then then it is just like candy floss.

Whilst it might look good, that does not mean it has connected. Far from it.

I was working with a hotel, a delightful hotel. The owner is a gentleman and has a huge thirst for feedback. Everything he says is a question. It is an admirable desire to continue to learn well into his 70s.

He had spent a lot of money with an agency on refreshing his brand. Much of it looked good but then came the words. In big bold letters, the catch phrase was: "We promise you a good night's sleep".

If ever you find yourself in an advisory role, it can be challenging to give true feedback, but the alternative is far worse. Inevitably, doing the 'right thing' will be more difficult.

I read the line and spotted a flaw immediately. He was so proud of it. Eventually, the inevitable, "What do you think?" and that tricky moment.

I told him that I thought the photography was beautiful, the font and branding were good but not outstanding and that the tag line would not work. He looked surprised but a man always wanting to learn was not going to fall at the feet of ego.

"How do you mean, Conor?"

You can build a beautiful hotel. You can give me the most silent room with the best bed, the softest sheets and wonderful soundproofing. You can have blackout blinds, air conditioning and the best bathroom ever. But, if I am an insomniac, if I am not well, if I am agitated, if I am up early, you cannot promise me a good night's sleep. All you can do is offer me the most wonderful room, but you cannot control how I do or do not sleep.

When you write, you can only promise what you can control. If you do not, there is always a danger, not of a protest march, but of sleep-deprived guests looking for their money back.

100 Bedrooms

Writing the above hotel story reminded me of another missed message.

Another owner, another day. This time, I was travelling by train and enjoying the luxury of time to think, for coffee, to sit back, and to work a little, to enjoy the view and to remember the childhood excitement of first journeys.

There is still something majestic about a train pulling into a railway station, especially a smaller one. This destination was a little smaller than the big city stations, so the bystanders' focus was always sharp.

I got off the train and headed for a taxi. Overarching the entire exit was a giant poster advertising my client's hotel. The line stood out but, for me, not for the right reasons. It said: "The city's largest hotel with 100 bedrooms".

I could hear myself sigh. It was muscle-flexing and it did not show warmth. Most of all, it was talking to itself.

I was not there to discuss their marketing or message, but it niggled away at me because it was not what the hotel was about. On the contrary, the hotel was understated and exceedingly good. Nonetheless, the message was detached from the reality and it was doing a little harm.

Over lunch, the owner mentioned the recent marketing exercise and then stopped himself, saying: "Now that I think of it, I should have checked it with you".

He had opened the door and I told him I had noticed it on my way in. Inevitably, I triggered the question: "And what did you think?"

I asked him why he thought the primary message ought to be the number of bedrooms. He did not really have a reason other than the agency he commissioned told him it was right. Again, I asked on what basis they had produced this. His answer was a rude awakening for me and for him: "They told me my message should be about dominating the local market".

Supressing my true reaction so that I would not be politically incorrect, I asked him if it might have been better to talk to the guest rather than terrorising the competition, if that was their aim?

He asked me to elaborate.

"Being the biggest is not really relevant. It is arrogant and tells me nothing that helps me. You see, I do not really care about 99 of your bedrooms. I care about one. Mine."

Many years ago, I learnt a simple maxim that this little story revived. When we are communicating with anyone, in any way, there are three words we can use: I, We, and You.

The goal is to use 'You' 80% of the time.

Where you must use 'I', you can always substitute it for 'We' – leaving 1% for the rare occasion you will have to use 'I'.

The next time he was revisiting the railway station sign, I asked him if he might change the focus to 'Your room' rather than the 99 I would have no interest in. It did not take long.

A week later, he sent me a photo of the new railway station poster. A beautiful photo, two words, one brand: "Your room".

It worked.

If you have an important point to make, don't try to be subtle or clever.
Use a pile driver. Hit the point once. Then come back and hit it again.
Then hit it a third time – a tremendous whack.

Winston Churchill

17: Insincerity

What we say and what we mean are often different. Most of us have a goal, an outcome we want but when that motivation is disguised, and employs humility, it becomes superficial humility. Whilst it might not be exposed at the time, it will be exposed down the road.

If we chase the things that 'tickle our ears', we'll probably end up finding out that they're going to 'torture our lives'.

Craig D. Lounsbrough

A Postcard

Back in the day when postcards adorned the shop front of every seaside store, postcards were an essential purchase. They started out life as heavily-filtered images of a non-existent paradise and before long, the industry added in cartoons. One such cartoon caught my young eye and though funny, it has stayed with me as a great way of making a point.

Beautifully drawn, the cartoon showed a young man standing beside his brand-new sports car. In his excitement, having just taken delivery, he went a little too fast, lost control and crashed into a tree. The car appeared to be hugging the tree, such was the perfect distribution of damage. But the caption made the cartoon:

It takes 4,000 bolts to hold a sports car together and just one nut to dismantle it.

Superficial Humility is not Humility

Paul Kimmage, journalist, is a friend and a man who likes to listen. Often, good listeners are people of few words and their words are worth listening to. Social media has become a part of a necessary arsenal for people in business today and how they express themselves is their opportunity to reflect who they are in a way they are free to choose.

On Twitter, there is an almost naked transparency to the title people self-anoint with. They can proclaim to be this or that. We see exaggeration, ego, pride, and humility. Humility is an attractive trait, in the same way that arrogance will make most of us bristle.

I like to read Paul's tweets, knowing how well he writes and how tightly he writes about his subject.

On Twitter, we have a lot of space to write a brief description about who we are. Sometimes, less is more powerful. Paul Kimmage's self-made description should be a challenge to anyone who writes. He manages to paint a potent picture in just two words: 'Christy's son' .

But my point about Paul and Twitter is wider. He is a brave man who gets to the heart of the matter he writes about and is driven by a search for the truth, rather than the story. The story emerges from the former.

One night, I read another short line that was also at the heart of one of Paul's articles. It said, "Superficial humility is not humility" and so much of our communication falls headfirst into this category. The kind that says, "We must meet for coffee", which really means, "Can I come to see you and persuade you to do what it is I want from you?".

It is so clichéd it already assumes I drink coffee. You would stand out more if you suggested tea instead. At least, I would notice.

A Late 'Phone Call

For some unexplained reason, my desk still had a dinosaur land-line that was gathering dust. On night, around 9.00 pm, I was deep in the middle of writing an article. Suddenly, the telephone sprang into life and its harsh tone startled me. I was almost afraid to answer it.

It had to have been several years since it last kicked into life.

I answered it and, in my mind, this call seemed to come from some very remote outpost deep in South America. The combination of a long day and intense focused writing had exhausted the last of my energy. It was dark and the winter's night was persuading me to relax.

"Good morning, Kenny. How are you today?" came the voice over the crackling broken line.

I was trying to move my thinking away from the confusion of the article, the unexpected harsh ring tone and this man saying "Good morning" on a sharp frosty night. "Sorry?" was my reply.

"I did do say gooooood morning, Kenny. So I do wish you a gooooood morning."

I was getting cross. It was a call centre and I had a deadline to deliver. My thought train had been de-railed.

"And Kenny, how are you?"

It was time to embrace the moment and seize the opportunity. Introducing my reply, I gave a loud long sigh and my response went something like this: "I am so glad you asked me that question. So glad. In fact, it is incredibly kind of you, thoughtful and caring".

I could hear an uncomfortable shuffling in some sun-kissed tropical call centre.

"Sorry, Kenny, what?"

I told him that I was simply about to respond to his incredibly thoughtful question.

"Which question, Kenny?"

"The one where you asked me how I am."

"Oh yeah, yeah, that one. Go ahead."

I paused, knowing the script did not cater for this.

"Well, I am doing reasonably OK under the circumstances. My health is not good. The heating is broken in my house. I lost my job and I have no money. I cut my hand this morning and I am not sleeping well. But I do appreciate you calling and your concern. I will get over it."

I could hear him clearing his throat. I could hear papers rustling and then the very distinct tone of someone covering the mouthpiece as they filled their colleagues in on this crazy man.

With that, he was gone.

As Paul Kimmage said, "Superficial humility is not humility".

Visible and Invisible Messages

Communication is a tool that we use to influence others and bring about change in their attitudes, amongst many other reasons. What we communicate is always the outcome and product of our thoughts and, more importantly, our decisions.

Sometimes, if we give way to our emotions, it will not be long before we regret the outcome. Whilst we are always free to choose, we are not free from the consequences of our actions.

Overt or covert misuse of communication can be a dangerous thing.

Cats do not like going back into the bag and bolted horses do not return either.

Disguised false communication is dangerous; so too is overt angry writing.

A Write Queen

She had just opened her splendid and luxurious country house right on the seashore, and it looked beautiful in the highly-polished photos. If ever the interior reflected the owner, this was it. Both were elegant, both had a gentle whiff of superiority and both displayed the finer things in life.

The messages were seductive, and drew you in as if you would be meeting and living with minor royalty.

It was a big promise and so alluring that you felt you needed to just prove it a little bit.

For such a new addition to the hospitality and country house landscape, it had a lot of reviews. A deeper look might just confirm the grandeur.

Scrolling down through the many satisfied guests, a few similarities began to appear – even if they hid beneath a thin layer of camouflage. A little doubt turned into a big suspicion and then it was all over.

You see, there was one word used a little too often in many of the reviews. Unfortunately, the spelling of that word was wrong and, it seems, no less than 22 brand new guests spelt it wrong too.

Isn't it always the unimportant things we communicate that can unseat us?

All in His Eyes

His eyes always gave the impression that he was owned by some strange dark entity. No matter how he looked at you, you were unsettled and often wondered if he was considering having you for his next dinner. Still, he spoke well, could be funny, tough, and charming. But those eyes.

Sometimes our instincts overpower our logic. Sometimes we need to listen to them. He was an extraordinarily successful businessperson and enjoyed the trappings of his success and, over lunch, he told me a story. He was fond of money and it dominated every tale. He was Mr. Cash. One story stood out. It was designed to make sure his authority and strength were all powerful.

He was owed money and was having difficulty getting paid, though it was not a large debt. He wound up the pressure and clearly enjoyed it. Eventually, he got paid – by cheque. And then the cheque bounced.

In a strange way, he enjoyed that too. It gave a sense of permission for what he was about to do. He was about to communicate in a very extreme way.

He knew exactly where this poor unfortunate lived. He knew his route to work, and he knew he had a great reputation for being an honest man, a pillar of his community and a man who gave his time freely to worthy causes.

He went to the printers and enlarged the cheque, complete with the bank's red 'unpaid' stamp, onto a roadside sign. He ordered 20 and later that night, he placed them at every roundabout the man would drive through.

His message was clear, but nobody remembers who wrote the cheque. They do remember who tried to humiliate him.

Unseen in the background, Fate was quietly slipping lead into the boxing-glove.

P.G. Wodehouse, Very Good, Jeeves

18: RESPONDING

Talking is a great skill, listening another – but few consider responding as a skill. It is our reaction to something that paints a powerful picture of who we are. Interviews are a good example of where we can use this art form to its best effect. Often, it is not the question that reveals most; it is the reaction and response that gives real insight.

On the other hand, beware, because if you interview using the stock questions, you are going to get stock answers.

They tell you nothing.

A response, be it written or verbal, is a decision you can control. That is easy when it is a simple transaction but far more difficult if it is a subject that tugs at our emotions. Often, if we are making a complaint, what we are really saying is emotional. Think about it, that vague statement, "I am not happy with your service standards" can really mean "I do not like you".

Once emotions come into play, there is a challenge in how you respond, not to manage your emotions, but to manage yourself. The possibilities are many, but the wrong choice will leave a lasting memory.

Urgent and Important

I was at a meeting with a group of people with a wizardry with words. They were bright, creative, and very engaging. My furious note-taking was not to record the minutes or even to look especially diligent. It was just that I tried to capture so many new phrases that were gold dust to my young ears. I could not keep up and lost about 80% of what I was trying to save but I do remember this one.

Never confuse urgent with important.

Often, important trumps urgent and the urgency we might feel in needing to reply to an angry letter may be best served by thinking whether it is more important not to.

Call Yourself a Professional?

When we are young, we are fearless. When we are fearless, we do not think of the consequences of our decisions. That is also a part of the joy of youth; we do not worry too much. In middle age, that all changes and the balance shifts, or at least we hope so.

Even the person suddenly arrested by the police is given exactly this caution: "Anything you do say may be written down and used in evidence against you".

Unfortunately, a tidal wave of emotions can hide the sensible thing.

A story was racing around the bush telegraph. A brand had been very naughty, and had been a little too creative in its marketing, positioning, self-made awards and imaginary positive social media praise

The story got picked up by a newspaper and it was published. But what nobody knew was that the paper only published half the story. A trap was being laid.

Part 1 asked whether the complaints and allegations were true. It put the brand's spokesperson in a difficult position. They were a little too quick in their reply. They went on record to defend the allegation.

It was a gamble.

A few days later, the newspaper printed part 2. It included the spokesman's rebuttal but then the writer produced the evidence.

It was awful, undeniable and factual.

A close friend of mine was about to do some work with this company. He is a remarkably successful man of absolute integrity and with an enviable reputation.

Objective to his core, disregarding the bandwagon parade, he was not about to add to the lynching. By coincidence, a former client, with whom he has a long-standing relationship, got in touch wanting his expertise. He had to take this assignment. Loyalty matters even if it was less rewarding.

He wrote to the naughty company and declined the assignment and went to great lengths to explain that he had an enduring loyalty to his former client. From an ethical point of view, he was not comfortable even if it were a project he would have enjoyed.

Then the fuse blew.

Sometimes, we can all be guilty of adding 2 + 2 and getting 6.

Unfortunately, the spokesperson who had denied building an uneven playing field was the very same person who was reading his "Thank you but no thank you" letter.

It hit a nerve, but the reply did not come immediately, it came close to midnight.

My friend's name was spelt wrong and the first line was the sound of an airborne Sidewinder missile. It said: "Yeah right, you really think I believe that??? Do you think I am stupid???".

He read on, curious as to where this missile would land.

He did not have to wait long.

As the missile flew, it gathered heat, anger, and power and then it exploded.

"Call yourself professional?????"

He wondered why the tally of question marks was increasing with each sentence.

But the missile missed and simply had no impact on its intended target.

To this day, he laughs about it and tries to remember how many typos and errors he counted.

And why does he laugh?

He never once called himself 'professional'.

That too went out on the bush telegraph and, as with all gossip, grew more legs than a millipede.

Sometimes, you are better off not to grant their wish for a fight. Whilst you might regret what you said, you will never regret saying nothing.

An Interview

I was an external interviewer for a friend some years back.

In came a man of incredible energy, a huge smile, a man in a hurry. He spoke well, listened well, and made great eye contact.

He was winning us over and he made it to the short second round list. The bookies would have had him as odds on favourite.

The second interview came and went, and he did very well. He was in touching distance of the prize – and then it fell apart.

Unsolicited, and with the best intentions, he decided to write to the chief executive as a pre-emptive strike that might just help him stand out from the crowd.

It did.

It went something like this.

Dear Kieran,
Kieran, how the devil are you?
That last meeting was great fun and I really enjoyed myself. Thank you.
I think you would be amazing guys to work with and I'd say we would
all have great fun on mission 'grow those sales'.
Give me a bell when you want me to start and let us get that ball rolling.
Cheers for now.
Peter

Oh dear. It is imperative we know our strengths and vital that we recognise our weaknesses, especially our communication weaknesses.

My Dream Job

I am not a gambler, but I gambled.

I was in a job, working for some nice people, but I hated my job.

The more I went in, the worse it got. My fault entirely, one of those important and useful career wrong turns that teaches us so much.

It was time to go.

This time, I would make the right move.

There were plenty of opportunities, the economy was buoyant, and it was more difficult to pick the right move that had a logical basis.

One night, I sat down with pen and paper. I was going to write down the criteria for my perfect job. The list was not long but there were five non-negotiables.

I went on the interview circuit and it was ripe with offers. Some were a definite "No", but others had appeal.

Back to my list. This time no compromise. A close fit was not good enough.

One Sunday, around this time, I read an interview with Mel McNally, one of Ireland's best-known interior architects, who specialised in hospitality design. His companies were extraordinarily successful, and his international reach was a success story.

As I read the interview, I realised that my five non-negotiables were flowing through this article.

There was no mention of McNally looking to recruit anyone with my background, but that was of no concern to me.

I wrote directly to him the next day and, a little boldly, said I would like to meet to discuss working with his firm. Suddenly, all the other semi-offers were less and less attractive. I wanted to work for this company, full stop.

After a week, I had not received a reply. My excitement was slowing down. The next day, I picked up the business section of the same paper and there, in a half-page advert was 'my' company advertising for what I believed to be my perfect skill set.

It was such an attractive position that my initial euphoria was tainted with despair.

The good news was that they had a perfect position for me. The bad news was that this advert was sure to attract a big response.

It did.

125 people applied for the job. That number was whittled down to a 'short list' of 25 for interview.

Soon, I got called for interview, but it was with an external recruiter. Excitement again turned a little sour. I wanted to meet the main man.

My interview was at 2:30 pm and it was made clear these would be short screening interviews.

I arrived early and went into a big anonymous waiting room with an eclectic collection of single chairs and an even more confusing collection of paintings and prints.

I counted six other people in the room.

At 2:30 pm on the dot, I was called in. The interviewer had a long sheet in front of him and I saw that each interview was allocated 15 minutes.

My interview was going well, very well. Easy when your true passion automatically comes out. But it was going well for another reason. Outside, in my mind, were the opposition. They would be anxious, impatient, and uncomfortable. My goal was to make that far worse. I succeeded. My 15 minutes ran to 45 minutes and I knew I had created a chaotic backlog that would show in thinly-disguised body language.

When I left the room, I could feel the daggers pinging off my back. To add fuel to the fire, I turned, looked at the entire room, smiled and said, "Good luck, everyone".

I really wanted this job.

The 25 were shortlisted to five. Then the five to two and then came the appointment. I had made it to the last two but being second was no good. I wanted this job.

The final interview came, and we got on well. There was a fly in the ointment. By now, I knew who the other candidate was. He was far better qualified for the role and rightly so. I was up against it.

As soon as the interview was over, I ran to my car, took out my pen and pad and I wrote something as simple as this.

Dear Mel,
I enjoyed meeting you again today.
At our meeting, you said the four most important things about this
appointment are A, B, C, and D.
I believe I can fulfil all of that as we discussed.
I look forward to meeting you again when you are ready.
Best wishes,
Conor

I got the job and they were six of the most rewarding, interesting, and educational years of my life.

Mel is a visionary and he was ahead of everyone throughout his career. Like all good bosses, he could be tough, but he was fair and a gifted natural teacher.

Not long after I started, I was in New York with Mel. We always did long days and nights and we were perpetual international motion. Late one night, we were having a nightcap.

Mel said to me, "Do you know why you got the job?"

I said, "Yes. I do".

Putting a $50 bill on the table, he said, "Really? Take out a $50 bill. If you are right, you take mine. If I am right, I take yours".

I told him I got the job because of the follow-on note. I took Mel's $50 bill and he laughed.

If you stop to think, it is not that difficult to be a real alternative and to respond when most will do what everyone else does, which is often nothing.

19: DIFFICULT CONVERSATIONS

Difficult conversations are difficult, but it is our perspective that makes them so, often unnecessarily.

Inevitably, these kinds of conversations are never about getting the facts or even getting to the truth. They are about our goal, how we interpret the situation, our hidden agenda, and how we see the moral question, right and wrong.

What we want out of conversation is not obvious. That can lead to false conclusions, depending on how the other person is positioned in tone, attitude, and body language. Not only is that dangerous, it can misguide us because we are often wrong in the heat of these situations. Other people's intentions are complex and the first mistake we can easily make is to start the conversation with the awful phrase, "I know exactly where you are coming from".

We do not.

The starting point with any difficult conversation is to know exactly what you have come into the room to do. From there, it is a good idea to set out a sincere desire to understand. That means to understand their perspective, as well as explain yours.

Naturally, if emotions storm in, the cloudy mist will distort the view and perspectives will instantly change.

It is easy to jump to a conclusion that most difficult conversations are about disciplining someone or, worse still, asking them to leave a company. Yes, they are a part of it but there are many types of difficult conversation and it is almost impossible to have them without those emotions jumping on to the stage too.

A useful guide to help might be:

- Be prepared. Know as many facts as you can and avoid starting with any presumptions;

- Have a clear outcome that is your guiding light and goal;
- Start by clearly explaining why you have come into the room;
- Do not waste time on the build-up and a scenic introduction. Get to the point;
- Listen. Then listen again and again;
- Understand what is not said;
- Stay calm;
- Stay focused;
- Stay human. These are people, not machines.

Hard Work

I was upstairs in the meeting room with the door open. Outside, a young man was moaning to a colleague. Every second sentence was "This is hard". He was putting more energy into complaining than getting the job done. We could all replay our youth through his words.

At his early age, a horizon was no more than eight hours and the weekends were heaven.

Robert, a young manager, and a man in a hurry to get to the top, is a man who works hard, extremely hard. His office was beside my eavesdropping perch. If I could hear the young man's moaning, so too could Robert. I waited for this to play out. It did.

"David, come here." It was not really a question. The tone was a clear command.

"David, you have been moaning all morning. What is the problem?"

David was not old enough to see the potential tattoo he was about to leave on Robert's memory. He replied, "But Robert, I am tired, and this work is hard, very hard".

Robert did not waste another moment.

"And what do you get for this demanding work, David?"

"My wages", said a brooding David.

"That is right", said Robert. "Wages. And do you know why it is called 'work', David? Do you? Well, let me tell you. It is because it is hard. Work, David, is hard. That is why it is called work."

The Nicest People Ever

It can be tricky to work for a family business. Blood is thicker than water and often the focus is on managing your position rather than keeping your eye on the job.

I have worked for many family businesses. Often, they get a bad press, which is not always fair. Some of my happiest days were with the kindest people.

However, in one case, I really did not like my job. As time went on, I liked it even less. It was a spiral that was never going to be reversed.

It was an exceptionally good business, successful and well run, but it was not for me. I was not getting excited by the business in any way. But they were good people, particularly good people.

As the speed of the spiral increased, so too did my declining performance. I felt damned if I stayed and unsure about my future if I left. It was a dreadful rock and hard place. I prayed for the decision to be taken out of my hands. An abdication from doing the right thing.

Time passed and my dreadful demotivated performance had not heralded the inevitable dispensing with my services. I was disappointed. The euphoria of a Friday evening respite was matched by the sheer gloom of a Sunday night. The rollercoaster had to stop before madness set in.

The managing director was as close as one gets to commercial sainthood. Kind, patient, thoughtful and not a man to hurt a soul.

A call came. Would I meet with him that afternoon, along with some of his fellow directors?

I felt a mixture of fear and relief.

My hand went to straighten my tie and I felt myself bracing, straightening up and getting ready for the forthcoming execution.

I walked into his office and there were three of them sitting quietly, patiently and a little downcast. I was the most upbeat and, in my head, I had prepared my thoughts to give them forgiveness for what they were about to do. After some fidgeting, small talk and throat-clearing, the managing director began.

This was not his comfort zone and I felt guilty that I was responsible for putting him in this position.

"We wanted to have a word with you, Conor. And apologies for the short notice. For some time now, we have noticed that you are coming in a little late and leaving a little early. Also, your motivation and energy seem a little low and the great start you got off to when you joined seems to have faded a little."

Then there was silence, a long, uncomfortable pause. I was not sure whether this was inviting me to reply or whether I should stay quiet and let the verdict come.

The silence continued and I offered a neutral "I fully understand". It was the prisoner's way of saying "Pull the trigger".

More eyes to the floor and more discomfort and a little more small talk. I felt myself mumbling that they needed to just get on with it. That is when the shock came. A scenario I never predicted.

The managing director was live again.

"You see, the thing is, we understand that you seem flat, demotivated and all that goes with it. That is why we wanted to meet you and tackle this head on."

I thanked them and then.

"So Conor, if we can cut to the chase and we hope you will not mind us doing so, what we are trying to say is that we are worried about you and we want to know that you are OK."

I was stunned. This was not in the script. I did not know how to react, what to say or even how I felt. I was numb.

I left the office and tried to process the implications. There was nothing to process.

My future was in my hands.

Although they might have avoided a difficult conversation, my only memory of that meeting is one of incredible kindness, self-sacrifice and people who put people first and profit second.

Sometimes, the most difficult conversation does not have the obvious outcome. 'Difficult' can have a powerful moral compass a few layers below obvious.

The Mechanic

One of the most difficult conversations you can ever have is to tell someone that their job is being terminated.

In that position, you will learn a lot about who you are and whether empathy is part of who you are. For some, it is not.

Sean was a true gentleman, gentle in every way. Not a man to curse, to offend or to cause problems, at least not intentionally.

Reliable, punctual, and diligent Sean had loyalty and integrity in abundance. But Sean was not performing. He was in a sales role and I was his immediate manager. I was concerned and so too were the owners of the business.

We waited, we trained, we supported, and it had insignificant effect. It could not go on indefinitely, a decision was taken, and I was dispatched to break the bad news. It was deeply troubling, and I had no idea how I was going to deliver it.

Sean had no idea what was coming.

I asked Sean if he had time for a coffee and we set off to a cafe nearby. Sean was in great spirits and, as we walked, told me he always enjoyed our conversations. I felt like Judas.

I still had not figured out how I was going to give him this awful news. To make matters worse, he had just become a Dad and they were looking forward to buying their first house.

Coffee was awkward and more so because Sean saw this as a pleasant interlude. I was stalling.

Somehow, we got talking about cars and some new models. Sean's eyes widened and his speech accelerated. This was his happy subject. I said nothing.

He got more animated as he told me that he fixed something on his own car that the garage said was beyond repair. He had gifted hands and one story led effortlessly into another.

In all of this, I had no idea how to introduce my mission, let alone how to break the excited flow of stories. I had never seen this energy before.

Eventually, the stories fizzled out and I knew my time had come.

There was an uncomfortable pause and I hoped that my nervous toe tapping had not been seen. I was about to speak but Sean got there first.

"Conor, I am glad we went out for this chat and I appreciate your support and constant encouragement but I know my performance has not been fantastic and I do not want to let you or the company down. Talking to you just now made me realise that my heart is elsewhere, and I am not being true to myself."

I had no idea where this was going but I was not about to interrupt. But a little window had appeared, so I grabbed it.

"If you were to imagine your dream job, Sean, what would it be now that you have reflected a little?"

He did not stop for breath.

"A mechanic. Yes, a mechanic."

Another pause, the tone solemn, slow, and soft.

"Would you be mad at me if I were to leave the company? It is just that I know, deep down, I am not enjoying my role and I am scraping by every week."

I reassured him that his first loyalty was to himself and his family and that he must do what was right for him. He went to great lengths to tell me he did not want to let me down or be disloyal. I told him he was not doing anything wrong and his own fulfilment mattered more than anything.

He sighed and smiled as if the weight of the world had been removed. He resigned that afternoon and, to this day, never knew why we went for coffee.

Not only did Sean do well, at the last count, his garage was employing 15 people and growing.

I told my Dad this story shortly afterwards. When I finished, he said:

> There is no such thing as a lazy person. They are either
> sick or in the wrong job.

I found myself intuitively disagreeing. Over time, I realised he was right.

If you do not agree, ask Sean.

20: In Business

We spend so much of our life at work. We build friendships, we have arguments, we learn, and we remember. It is our daytime village and, just like our memories, work can leave a powerful imprint: good and not so good.

If our work is who we are, then it will be a successful career. However, if Sunday evenings are the gates to Hell and Friday evenings the beginning of 48 hours of euphoria, then you are in the wrong job.

How we behave at work does not reflect as much on us as it does on the company and its perceived brand values. That creates responsibility – for the company, its owner and its managers. And that responsibility is nowhere more visible than in the people the business employs.

No matter how good the company's processes, there is always a risk. The risk is created by perception and perception is created primarily by the interaction the customer has with the business's staff. Your people are the brand, your brand.

There are many complex definitions of a brand and most of them unintentionally muddy clear waters. My definition is simple:

A brand is what you think and feel about a business when you are not there.

As an employer, you can recruit for the function or to fit the brand. The clever approach must be to recruit both, since one is no good without the other.

Your brand has values and values are non-negotiable. Values are the principles that help you to decide what is right and wrong for your organisation, as well as guiding you how to act and behave in certain situations.

It is in our behaviour, especially when we step outside our professional self and into our emotional self that problems can occur.

Let me explain.

What is Marketing?

The purpose of marketing is remarkably simple. It is to create the desire to buy.

When we create our own marketing, it is not always easy to objectively assess the impact we are having on the person we want to read it. However, here are some simple but highly effective questions, thoughts, and ideas that will guide you:

- First, this applies to your website as well as your social media and advertising: Are you talking about yourself – or are you talking to the customer?
- Second, is your message clear? Is it trying to be clever?
- Third, are you competing? Or, are you clearly an alternative, a different choice?
- Four: If you are a real alternative, have you told me why?
- Five: Get to the point. Be short, be sharp, and be clear. Edit your message and when you are done, edit again;
- Six: Remember my ability to digest a message is a small window. Do not block it with unnecessary stuffing;
- Seven: Are you clear who are you want to talk to, and do you know where they are and how to get to them?

Finally, have you made it clear what the risk is to the customer of passing you by?

Out of Control Emotions

In business, it is easy to believe that anyone who is rich or successful has mastered managing their emotions and decision-making. They have not.

Sometimes, people make a lot of money very quickly, which can create its own problems.

Everybody wants to be recognised and it is nice to be nice and even nicer to have people treat you well. Doing the opposite creates problems and creating problems guarantees pain.

The bank business has moved from a very interactive and personal place into an online world where that touch is gone. It can be a difficult transition for an older generation built on relationships.

This bank employs thousands of people and the customer was a very wealthy man of property. He moves with speed and retirement is a word that means nothing. Over the years, he had built up many relationships as his business rocked from high to low, boom to the brink and back again. Overall, he was financially secure for life and his business grew and grew with some very astute decisions. Banks courted him and the newspapers followed him. He had a high profile.

One night, over dinner, he told the table a story.

He had bad service from his bank and a slow response. Eventually, for the man always in a hurry, he was put through to a middle manager. The fuse was already short, and it was not going to take much before the explosion came. The manager was not moving quickly enough and certainly did not seem to be in tune with the urgency. Real or imagined, he swears he heard a yawn – and his temper exploded.

The bank employee began to fight back and threatened to hang up if the customer continued to be rude.

He continued. The phone went dead.

The anonymous manager could not be traced but he was having none of it. There was a score to settle.

He was no longer caught up in the heat of the immediate issue. He was beyond that and intent on frying a bigger fish.

Eventually, he got through to a member of the top team and wanted to know the name of the person who had not given the best service ever. The executive declined to oblige; this was war.

His portfolio and borrowings were eye-watering figures that would keep mere mortals awake at night.

He called the senior executive back a few days later. In the meantime, he entertained the advances of competitor banks who were eager to have his business.

The senior banker took the call. It lasted seconds.

I have banked with you for 32 years. I am one of your biggest clients. I reflected on the tone of your yawning manager and I reflected on your dismissive attitude quoting the rule book. In the meantime, I invited all your competitors to meet me. As a man who lives by confidentiality and the rule book, I am sure you will understand that I am not in a position (he then yawned loudly) to tell you which of your competitors is now the proud owner of all my bank accounts. You are nothing but a bunch of amateurs. Goodbye.

Business is ebb and flow. We are ahead, we are behind, but we plough on. The bank survived the loss and, in time, will forget about it.

The customer will not – and the most dangerous part of all of this is that it took one person, rightly or wrongly, to dismantle 32 years of positive relationships.

That is the danger of emotion getting in the way of logic but people, even very wealthy ones, are not always logical.

And, to this day, given any opportunity, this story is told again and again.

Can I Book a Room Please?

I had an early start one morning and a lot to pack into one day. It was winter and the weather had been troublesome and unpredictable. I decided it was sensible to go the night before.

Right beside my place of work was a delightful hotel. It was winter Sunday night, so I assumed that they would have plenty of rooms and be grateful for business in the lowest part of their season.

I called the hotel. The frosty response matched the chilly winter air. Knowing they would be almost empty, I asked if they would have a room available for the Sunday night. "I will have to check" came the ice-cold response. Moments passed. They did. I asked if they could offer me a better rate than the website rate. The answer was memorable "No". No explanation, no warmth, just "No". This lady was not for turning.

I said that I would have to consider booking elsewhere if there was no movement. She replied with that dreadful phrase: "No problem".

I replied, "It is".

Of course, the difficulty with this was that the brand suffers. Whilst you will not remember the person, you will remember the event and that is the story that gets told.

It is always worth thinking of the useful line:

I will not remember what you said. I will remember how
you made me feel.

That is what I mean when I said a brand is what you think and feel about a business when you are not there.

Discussion is impossible with someone who claims not to seek the truth,
but already to possess it.

Romain Rolland, Above the Battle

Who Are You Talking to and Are You Wasting Time?

When we are young, time and horizons have quite different meanings. As we grow older, that changes. This is the difference between knowledge and wisdom.

In business, choosing how to use time, and especially in how we want to engage, connect, and communicate with our customers, is a precious art that rewards. With limited time, resources, and energy, it is a commodity that can be your greatest asset.

You have mastered your craft. You've lots of knowledge. You are good at what you do. You have a real value. But beware of:

- Wasting your time;
- Focusing on the wrong market;
- Underselling yourself, your knowledge and your expertise;
- Trying to please those you cannot please;
- Tyre-kickers, pretenders, and thinly-disguised illusory customers;
- Trying to sell to those who want what you have but do not value your knowledge, price, expertise, principles, and brand. Beware of trying to please pretenders;

- Wasting your time on those who will waste their own wasting yours.

Your work matters. Your brand is good. You have survived storms. You work hard. You add value. You matter. Keep going. But make sure you are always talking to the people who value what you do, see the benefit and do not deflect you.

Remember, no matter how exciting and wonderful your product or service is, there is no such thing as your market being everyone.

That is an impossibility and a rapid route to failure.

Watch Your Language

How you write reflects your brand and is an unofficial signature for your company. What you say, on behalf of your company, tells me about your outlook, attitude, standards, and values. If your brand promises one thing but you deliver another, the perfect white ceiling will not be noticed, the crack in it will.

Language is getting lazy. It is a mirror image of a society where machines have replaced people, computers replaced intellect, fast food has replaced cooking, and shorter words for better words.

When I was growing up, a person died. Later, they passed away. Now, they passed. It can only be time before that finds an easier version. Similarly, to take a sporting comparison, I grew up watching Manchester United. That changed to Man U and to supporters now it is simply 'United'.

Formal language has been replaced with informality, the trademark of a younger generation.

That is well and good if you are talking only to people of a similar generation. To older generations, brought up in a different time, it sends out a different signal.

There are four generations and there are differences between them. At the youngest end, you have Gen Z. They see Millennials as outdated and old. Above those are Generation X, Baby Boomers, and Traditionalists.

Traditionalists still hand-write letters, send birthday and Christmas cards, call rather than text and put an extremely high value on the interaction with staff in a hotel stay or a restaurant night out.

Effective communication adapts to the different generations' needs expectations and what they see as polite.

Let me give you an example.

A Little Too Casual

My late father was a Traditionalist and an exceptionally fine author. For him, words mattered and, being of his generation and former teacher, he would not be slow to correct.

Our family were together to celebrate a milestone birthday. Befitting the occasion, a splendid private dining room was chosen to match. It promised a lot and the decor was superb and matched by the fine gold thread of expensive uniform.

That was where the brilliance ended and the staff, though charming, were an exceptionally long way short in the fine art of real service.

They forgot side orders, brought the wrong wine, mixed up drinks and even presented us with somebody else's starters.

"Oh, never mind, I am sure we will figure out who ordered this stuff." 'Stuff' is an interesting word indeed for a fine dining dish.

My Mum was deep in conversation with her daughter and daughters-in-law. Another young girl appeared in an oversized uniform and stormed into the middle of their conversation with a loud "Hi guys, who's for drinks?".

My Dad did not say a word, but her loose language would not have gone unnoticed.

On the way out, my Dad, always generous, had a big tip for the 'Hi guys' girl. The young girl could see it coming and her excitement was obvious.

"Now young man, thank you for all the good stuff tonight. Good evening."

The puzzled look on her face said she did not get it – but is that not what training is all about?

It prompted me to write a brief note which is central to our work today and appears on the home page of our website.

Every night when the lights go down, the show is over. Another day is done. The next day, no matter what has gone before it, the show will have a new audience, often a first-time audience, and the new day's show must, at the very least, be better than the day before. The actors who will deliver the show are your people. If you do not invest in them in many ways, you will have an average show. After all, what is the point of a beautiful, comfortable, cosy theatre with great sets, great seats and great lighting, if the guys on stage have no idea what they are doing?

In many ways, you can learn much from the poor delivery of a marvellous promise.

Although it was a family celebration, the casual interactions were a long way off the brand promise. Language matters and if the brand promised elegance, discretion, high skills and more, the interaction should match. It did not. My Dad's point?

"Lovely cheerful people. OK service. Conversation fit for a burger joint."

Not long ago, I had the pleasure of writing an article about The Ritz Hotel, Piccadilly, London.

In it, I spoke at length with John Williams, MBE, the executive chef who has cooked for the most famous faces. We walked and talked and ended up in the most famous of private dining rooms. Casually, responding to my wide-eyed enjoyment of this majestic room, John said, "The food must match the room".

As my Dad would have said, "Indeed".

More Old School

Patrick was the Front Office Manager at a fine hotel that my parents really enjoyed. We had never met.

By coincidence, I was giving a workshop to a team from Patrick's hotel and I told a story with credit to my Dad.

Later that day, we were giving out a memento or two to all the participants. Some were my books, and some were my Dad's. The early birds had their pick and Patrick was in no doubt that he was having one of my Dad's. "A gentleman to his fingertips," Patrick explained, adding with incredible recall, memories of my Mum and Dad: the room number they preferred, my Dad's car and, most of all, their conversations. I was mesmerised by the interest Patrick had in my parents and his genuine fondness for them.

Then, the poacher turned gamekeeper: "Let me tell you a story, Conor".

I was listening carefully.

One day, your Dad asked me for something. I did not produce whatever it was he was looking for. When I came back to his room to deliver the bad news, he was not at all concerned – but he taught me a lesson that I live with today. He said, 'If you cannot say "Yes", then you cannot say "No". Instead, you must say, "Leave it with me".

It brought a silent tear to my eye because it was so typical of my Dad. This fine young man was the perfect student with the perfect memory.

Not long after, I told my Mum this story. Before I finished, she said, "And his name is Patrick. A gentleman".

It was a very brief encounter with me, but it is often the smallest things that have the biggest impact and I will bet you Patrick never imagined his story and kindness would live on in a little book.

I will make sure he knows.

My Dad would have liked that. Not only did Patrick remember the story, he recalled it with great precision.

And the lesson? If we want to learn, we need to listen. And if you want to get to the top, like Patrick, we need to listen with care.

21: Forget Me Not

The Very Last Word

I decided, after a considerable period of reflection, that it was time to enrich the small, mature, south-facing garden. There was a corner that seemed lonely, soulless, and without purpose. A carefully-chosen specimen would enrich this bleak, barren corner. With that, I plotted a route to my nearest source of wonderful gardening implements, along with their excellent collection of fine fauna, flora, and specimens for the smaller garden. Having successfully chosen a fitting new addition, it was time to complete the purchase and I bought a lifelong, handcrafted, fine-finished, ergonomically-designed, carefully-engineered, professional standard specialist digging tool, which effortlessly combined two complementary materials: steel and wood, with an excellent, angular, innovative cutting blade, which would aid the completion of this remedial project.

Or put it another way:

I bought a shovel and planted a tree.

The next time you communicate, remember to call a spade a spade, make the complex simple, and realise that you do not know what the other person is thinking

Confusion is a luxury which only the very, very young can possibly afford and you are not that young anymore.

James Baldwin, Giovanni's Room

ABOUT THE AUTHOR

Conor Kenny

Conor is the founder and principal of Conor Kenny & Associates, a multi-award-winning professional development and training company.

He is the author of:

- *It's Who I Am, Irish Times* Books of The Year, 2017;
- *Dancing at the Fountain, Irish Examiner* Books of the Year, 2016;
- *Sales Tales* ,2014.

He is a former fundraising volunteer for Debra Ireland and is a director and board member of The Rutland Centre (addiction treatment).

OAK TREE PRESS

Oak Tree Press develops and delivers information, advice and resources for entrepreneurs and managers. It is Ireland's leading business book publisher, with an unrivalled reputation for quality titles across business, management, HR, law, marketing and enterprise topics.

In addition, Oak Tree Press occupies a unique position in start-up and small business support in Ireland through its standard-setting titles, as well training courses, mentoring and advisory services.

Oak Tree Press is comfortable across a range of communication media – print, web and training, focusing always on the effective communication of business information.

Oak Tree Press, Cork T12 EVT0, Ireland.
T: + 353 86 244 1633 E: info@oaktreepress.com
W: www.oaktreepress.com / www.SuccessStore.com.